Catching Fish.

YOUR PRACTICAL GUIDE TO BEATING $1/$2 NO - LIMIT TEXAS HOLD'EM GAMES

A POKERSITES.COM GUIDE

WRITTEN BY EDWARD SCIMIA

TABLE OF CONTENTS

FOREWORD

Poker has exploded in popularity during the past decade – and so has poker literature. There are hundreds of poker books that are designed to teach you how to play like professional poker players, how to play against professional poker players, and how to understand the theory that underlies complex poker play.

But not every player wants to become a high-stakes professional. For many players, the end goal is a much more modest one – they want to be winners in low-stakes games, and nothing more. They want to go to the casino, play in a $1/$2 game, and know that in the long run, they'll come out on top. In fact, it's probably true that there are many more players who fit into this category than there are aspiring poker pros. After all, plenty of players would be content to enjoy the casual, social nature of these low-stakes games – as long as they can turn a profit at the same time.

Yet there are very few materials geared specifically towards beating live low-stakes no-limit hold'em games. Sure, plenty of books give a token chapter to the topic, telling you how easy it is to win in these games and pointing out a few adjustments to their advice that you can use against weaker players. But these books can be confusing to the new player, and using advice meant for tough games at a typical low-limit table can be counterproductive, or even dangerous.

When I began playing poker seriously almost a decade ago, limit hold'em was the dominant game. But despite the fact that I read several books on how to play, I found myself losing money in the small stakes online limit hold'em games that I heard were goldmines (and at the time, they really were). It wasn't until I picked up a book dedicated specifically to these games – the excellent *Small Stakes Hold'em* by Sklansky, Malmuth and Miller – that I was able to start beating these games the way I knew I was "supposed to" be able to do. Before reading a book that was devoted to explaining how to take advantage of the bad play in these games, I had no chance to beat them, for two reasons:

- I had fundamental errors in my poker thinking that prevented me from properly utilizing the advice presented in more advanced books.
- The material in more advanced books was geared towards beating tough opponents; while it is true that weaker opponents are easier to beat, the techniques for doing so are often quite different, especially if you want to fully exploit them.

Today, I believe that the same situation holds for many no-limit hold'em players who are trying to learn how to beat $1/$2 games (or other small stakes games, such as home games). Not only is most of the advice out there designed to help you beat tough opponents, it also assumes some level of knowledge in poker fundamentals – something sorely missing among most beginning (and many intermediate) poker players.

Hopefully, this book can fill that gap for the aspiring small stakes no-limit hold'em player. Every chapter and every piece of advice within is meant to help you beat a very specific type of no-limit game – the typical $1/$2 table at your local casino. It's a practical guide, light on math and theory whenever possible, and heavy on advice that is presented as simply as possible so that you can immediately use it to improve your game. While there is occasionally advice that could be used against the rare tough opponents you'll see even in small stakes games, the standard advice throughout this book is meant to help you beat bad poker players by taking advantage of the massive mistakes they'll make time and time again.

This book will not teach you how to battle against professional poker players, and the style of play advocated can be exploited by a sufficiently tough opponent. But at a $1/$2 table, the goal is not to play "perfect" poker – it's to play in a way that takes full advantage of the errors the majority of your opponents will be making. It'll also do so while giving you a grounding in poker fundamentals, which will help you immensely should you choose to read more advanced materials that will prepare you for playing in tougher, higher stakes games.

I hope this book gives you the confidence, skills and knowledge necessary to become a winning player in live no-limit games played for small stakes. Winning in these games isn't quite as glamorous as being a high roller who dominates the nosebleed tables in Macau or Las Vegas, but for 99% of poker players, winning at a $1/$2 table is a realistic goal that can turn every casino trip into a profitable venture.

Edward Scimia

GOOD LUCK
AT THE TABLES!

PART I: BASIC POKER CONCEPTS

EXPECTED VALUE

While this book is going to be very light on theory and math, there are a few key mathematical concepts that all poker players must know in order to be successful. One of these is EV, or expected value.

Every bet you make, in poker or in any other gambling game, has an expected value in terms of cash (or in a tournament setting, also in chips). The expected value of a bet is the amount of money you'd expect to win or lose on average if you made that bet an infinite number of times. While it may seem complex, EV is actually a very simple concept to utilize and understand. If you make +EV (positive expectation) gambles, you'll expect to win in the long run. If you make –EV (negative expectation) bets, you can expect to go broke.

One simple example is a coin flip. If we each bet $100 on a coin flip, with me winning should the coin lands on heads, and you taking the cash if the coin lands on tails. Assuming we have a fair coin, 50% of the time you'll win $100, and 50% of the time you'll lose $100. In the end, you'll come out exactly even – your expectation is $0.

But we can change things so that you win. What if I have to bet $150 against your $100? Now you're losing $100 half the time, but the other half you win $150. Obviously, playing this game will make you a lot of money, but exactly how much money will you make per coin flip? The calculation looks something like this:

(.5 * $150) – (.5 * $100)

$75 - $50 = $25

You'll make, on average, $25 for every time we play this game. Very lucrative! But how does this relate to poker?

In poker, it is rarely possible to calculate our EV exactly. We don't know exactly what our opponents are holding, which means we don't know exactly what our odds of winning a hand are at any given time. We certainly can't know exactly whether or not our opponents will fold to a bluff, or how many bets we'll make on later rounds if we hit a draw. In these situations, we must use our experience and intuition to estimate the probabilities involved and make decisions.

Some examples are simpler, though. Say we have the nut flush draw on the turn against a single opponent who has put us all in. We'll have to call our last $100 to win a pot that already has $500 in it. For whatever reason, we feel confident that we can win if and only if we hit one of our nine outs to a flush draw, but that all nine of those outs will win the hand for us. We are clearly an underdog, and for many beginners, that's enough to tell them to fold.

But the truth is, that's not nearly enough! Even though we are way behind in the hand, we don't have to win the pot 50% of the time to break even – in fact, we only need to win one out of six times, thanks to the tremendous 5-1 pot odds we're being laid. Our flush draw will come in approximately 19.5% of the time, and when it does, we win $500. The other 80.5% of the time, we lose $100. Let's try that formula again:

(.195 * $500) – (.805 * $100)

$97.50 - $80.50 = $17

Every time we call that bet, we profit $17. It may feel risky, and losing that hand a few times may make some players timid to call such large bets, but the key is to avoid being results oriented. If we play this situation over and over again, we will make a profit, even though we're usually losing the hand.

The ability to understand this is a key factor that separates good poker players from poor ones. You cannot expect to win at poker if you're afraid to go after long shots when the odds justify it. You must take every +EV bet available and avoid –EV bets whenever possible. Only by doing this can you show a profit over the course of your poker career.

WHY POSITION MATTERS

One of the most critical concepts in poker – and one that's badly misunderstood by weak or novice poker players – is that of position. In poker, position refers to where you are in relation to the dealer button which decides which player acts last on most rounds of betting. The two players to the left of the button are the small and big blinds, and the next position is "under the gun;" the last player to act is known as being "on the button."

Being in late position – generally, on the button or one seat off the button – is a huge advantage. When you are in late position, you get to see every player in front of you act before you need to make a decision, and in poker, information is power. You'll know how many players are going to be in the pot, and if any players have shown strength by raising. If there are no players in the pot in front of you, you can attempt to steal the blinds. Should a lot of people call but not raise, you can play a lot of speculative hands, knowing that you'll act last on all of the later rounds.

Conversely, being in the blinds or under the gun puts you in bad position throughout the hand. If you make bets, the players behind you get to decide how to react to your aggression; if you try to check and encourage them to act first, they always hold the option of checking behind you and seeing a free card. A lot of your weapons are taken away from you in early position, as you're at a constant disadvantage. True, in the blinds, you'll get to act last on the first round of betting. But the fact that you must act first after the flop and the money you are forced to pay before seeing your cards more than make up for that small preflop edge.

How should this affect your play? First and foremost, your starting hand selection will be impacted tremendously by your position at the table. From early position, you won't be able to play quite so wide a variety of hands; weaker, more speculative hands will leave you with too many tough decisions to make later. Again, this is less true in the blinds, where you've already put money in the pot, but even in the blinds you must be extremely cautious if your opponents have made raises in front of you. From other early positions, we can't afford to play speculatively, as raises behind us would make us throw our hands away.

As you move into middle position, more hands become open to you, as you've started to gain some information. Since there are fewer players behind you, you're less afraid of a raise, and have some idea how many players will be in the pot going forward. You might be able to get away with playing some hands that are weaker, especially if a few players are in the pot and your hand is one that plays well against multiple opponents (like small suited connectors or small pairs).

Finally, in late position, you can play a wide variety of hands if there hasn't been a raise in front of you. After all, you can be reasonably sure that you're unlikely to face a raise behind you, and you know exactly how many players are in the pot. If nobody is in the pot yet, you can often try to steal the blinds; if many players have limped in, you might be able to play almost any hand that has value in a multiway pot.

Post-flop, playing in later position gives you even more information, which leads to a bigger edge for you. You'll have the option of closing the action by just calling or checking, or choosing to be more aggressive. It's very hard to gain control of a hand from a strong player in position, as they have much more control over the size of the pot.

Is there any good news for a player in early position? Well, if you're the first to act postflop, you do have the first chance to bluff at the pot. If you're in a spot where the first player to bet is likely to take down the pot, you'll be happy to go first. The rest of the time, you'll wish you were in position – which is why we'll recommend playing as many hands as possible when you have position on your opponents, rather than the other way around.

AGGRESSION AND FOLD EQUITY

Almost anyone who offers poker advice will tell beginning players that they need to be more aggressive. However, it's not always clear what exactly this means. For many players, gaining a handle on what constitutes proper aggressive play is what turns them from breakeven players into winners.

In poker, we can talk about players being either passive or aggressive. Passive players tend to call bets; aggressive players tend to bet and raise. In most cases, aggressive play is superior to passive play. Despite this, most weak players tend to play very passively, and often see aggressive players as wild maniacs.

This is because passive play feels very safe, and comes naturally to players who are risk adverse. By playing passively, pots tend to stay smaller and there is less risk of allowing the aggressive players to raise. This may give the passive player a sense of control over the hand.

But for the most part, it's the aggressive players who are in control, and the passive players who are just along for the ride! The key here is that aggressive players, by betting and raising, are giving themselves two ways to win a pot. They could have the best hand, but they could also win if their opponents fold to their bets. The chance a player has of winning a pot by getting their opponents to fold (or more accurately, the share of the pot that represents) is known as their fold equity. Aggressive players often have great fold equity against players who are willing to fold; meanwhile, since a call never provides you with any immediate fold equity, passive players rarely have any fold equity at all.

This does come with some risks. An aggressive player stands to lose more when they go to the end with a second-best hand, and leaves themselves open to reraises and check-raises. However, the large pots they win when they do have the best hand more than makes up for those minor drawbacks. In tough, tight games, aggressive players will pick up tons of small pots without a fight by betting other players off of their hands. In looser games with multi-way pots featuring several players going to the river hand after hand, the aggressive players will earn more than enough bets from the other players when they win to make up for the bets they lose on the occasions when another player beats them at showdown.

That last sentence is part of the key to aggressive play. It's not wild, mindless aggression – at least not for most players. Aggression paired with smart decisions when it comes to picking your starting hands and knowing when to fold is the key to winning at poker. Aggressive players are willing to fold when they don't expect to make a profit; often, their decisions are between raising and folding, with calling never becoming a consideration at all.

This is why most beginners are advised to play a style commonly known as TAG, or tight-aggressive. This style is a basic blueprint to beating your average, unskilled opponents that populate most low-limit games. You start with strong starting hands, aggressively bet and raise, fold when prudent, and take down huge pots by getting lots of calls with your strongest hands. The TAG style can be employed in limit or no-limit, and will generally be successful at most levels (though adjustments must be made when playing against strong and tricky players). As players become stronger, some switch to a LAG (loose-aggressive) style, especially in no-limit. However, these players are still using aggression as their main weapon; in many cases, these players might even be more aggressive than their TAG counterparts.

Aggression allows you to control hands and put pressure on your opponents. It gives you many ways to win a hand beyond simply having the best hand, while also guaranteeing the maximum profit when you do win at showdown. Simply put, aggression is a necessary part of winning at poker, and something that every player must learn to use if they want to make a profit during their poker career.

POT ODDS AND IMPLIED ODDS

Here's another one of those spots where we're going to have to get into some math – don't worry, it's nothing terribly complex. However, both pot odds and implied odds are critical to determining how to proceed in a given hand. Without an understanding of both, it is nearly impossible to be a competitive player against even very weak opponents.

This isn't to say that you should rely only on numbers; you'll have to use your experience, intuition and psychology to figure out how strong a hand you think your opponents have, or how they're likely to react to a big bet. But at the end of the day, that's only part of the equation, and you'll need to understand a few basic concepts about odds to make good decisions and play winning poker.

Pot odds are perhaps the most basic mathematical concept in poker. Pot odds are the odds given to you by the money that's already in the pot, compared to how much you'd have to bet to stay in the hand. For instance, if there's $100 in the pot, and you'd have to call $10 to see a showdown on the river, your pot odds would be 10-1.

Pot odds are the main reason why it's often right to chase long shot hands, and why simply knowing that your opponent probably has you beat isn't enough to fold. For instance, you might have a weak hand like third pair with no kicker against one opponent, the kind of hand that can only beat a bluff. But you read your opponent to be strong, so you're almost certain he has you beat; in fact, you'd say there's only a 5% chance he's bluffing. He bets into you on the river. What should you do?

The only correct answer is: you don't have enough information yet! Your decisions should always take pot odds into consideration. Let's say the pot has $500 in it, and your opponent is betting $20 on the river. You'll lose $20 95% of the time, but the other 5%, you take down $500 by catching his bluff. Is it worth it? The math looks like this:

$$(.05 * \$500) - (.95 * \$20)$$

$$\$25 - \$19 = \$6$$

You'll make $6, on average, by calling in this spot! However, even if you're that confident in your read, you shouldn't call without being certain the math is in your favor; change that pot to just $300, and while calling is tempting, you'd actually lose $4 each time you called.

Pot odds are great when you know you'll get to see the rest of the cards in the hand for one bet – either on the river, or when you are put all-in earlier in a hand. However, when you are earlier in a hand, sometimes using only pot odds can make you play too conservatively. For instance, you may have a flush draw on the flop in a $30 pot, and need to pay $10 to see the next card. Your pot odds are only 3-1, and you only have a 19% chance to make the flush on the turn – a little worse than 4-1 against.

But that doesn't tell us the whole story. If you make your flush, you can expect to collect extra bets on the turn and the river, and we have to take that into account too. We call these potential extra bets our implied odds – money we can assume we'll collect should we make our draw, even though it's not in the pot yet.

Unlike pot odds, implied odds are an inexact science. We can't know for sure who will put how much money in the pot on later rounds; instead, we have to do our best to estimate. Things that will help make implied odds larger include a larger number of betting rounds to come (a draw on the flop can collect money on the turn and river when it hits, but a draw on the turn will only collect on the river), a larger number of players in the hand, weaker opponents who are less likely to read our hand, and disguised hands that are difficult to read. On the other hand, experienced players are less likely to pay us extra bets, and obvious draws that come in with scary cards on the board tend to push our implied odds down too.

Sharp readers might have figured something out in the discussion about implied odds. If we have to factor in the chance that our opponents might pay out more when we win, shouldn't we also consider the fact that we might make a second best hand, and pay off our opponent? This relates to a more advanced concept known as reverse implied odds. The idea is fairly simple; sometimes our odds aren't as good as they appear, because we may put more bets into the pot going forward with a hand that will lose at showdown. Essentially, implied odds make us want to play hands that could improve on future rounds and catch our opponents by surprise, while reverse implied odds make it worse to play hands that aren't going to collect a lot from opponents, but might force us to pay off an opponent with a better hand.

In no-limit poker, pot odds are critical in situations where the stacks are short or players will be all-in; in deep-stacked games, implied odds (and reversed implied odds) are dominant. Keeping these factors in mind will prevent you from making huge mistakes – whether it's chasing hands you should be folding, or folding hands that should be making you money.

ADJUSTING TO YOUR OPPONENTS

When you play poker, you'll face a myriad of different opponents across the felt. Rarely will you meet two players who are exactly alike; each will bring their own experiences and skills to the table, and much of the strategic and tactical depth of poker comes from figuring out how to exploit each individual's playing style.

Of course, if you're playing $1/$2 No Limit Texas Hold'em at your favorite casino, chances are that you'll rarely spend enough time playing against most of your opponents to get to know their games to that level. Instead, you're going to have to quickly come to some general conclusions about their play that will help you adjust to their style and exploit their tendencies as much as possible.

In order to do that, we need to have a way to classify our opponents. The simplest way to do this is by using the two classical measures of poker style to come up with a few archetypes. Those two measures are:

Tightness: This is a measure of how many hands a player chooses to play. A tight player plays few hands, while a loose player plays many hands.

Aggressiveness: This is a measure of the types of actions a player tends to make during a poker hand. An aggressive player is more likely to bet or raise during a hand; a passive player is one who will generally make calls rather than lead the action themselves.

Between these two measures, we can generally classify players into the four different categories. The following is a quick guide to each player type; later in the book, we'll often refer to these player types and make suggestions about how to adjust your play to them when necessary.

Loose-Passive

Loose-passive players will be the most common opponents you face in live $1/$2 games. These players will tend to play far too many hands, with little regard to position. In addition, they'll rarely take advantage of the times when they do make strong hands unless they feel their hand is nearly unbeatable; however, they'll often call down anytime they hit any part of the board, with little regard for pot odds or other considerations.

If there's one player you should like to play against again and again, it's the loose-passive player. Since these players are so common at the lower levels of live casino play, this book is generally going to give you advice geared towards beating loose-passive players.

Loose-passive players are often known as "calling stations." Many mediocre players actually dislike playing against these players, due to the fact that they rarely fold; as such, they'll hit their draws more often and stick around to improve in hands where better players would likely have folded.

However, it's important to remember that the goal of poker is to win as much money as possible – not to win as many hands as possible. Yes, loose-passive players will sometimes hit their miracle card on the river, apparently robbing you of a big pot. However, putting lots of money into the pot when you're behind is not a winning strategy; in the majority of cases, they'll simply be donating money to you. Don't let the frustration of the occasional losses to these players make you forget that these are your most profitable opponents. Play well, and your winrate against the typical loose-passive player will be tremendously high.

Tight-Passive

A tight-passive player is one who plays very few hands, and in addition, tends to play them passively. One sure sign that you're up against a tight-passive player – also known as a "rock" – is in the way they talk about poker at the table. They'll complain about how they never get a hand, about how they constantly get sucked out on by the "maniacs"

at the table. If there's one line that best exemplifies the mindset of the tight-passive player, it's "I need to move up to a higher limit, where they'll respect my raises!"

The truth is that tight-passive players would do even worse against strong opponents than against weak ones, but don't tell them that. Tight-passive players are another group against which you should expect to make a solid profit, though perhaps not at quite the rate you will against the loose-passive players. These players will generally fold far too often; that's very exploitable (you'll want to make continuation bets and semi-bluffs against these players mercilessly), but they're much less likely to ship their entire stack to you with bottom pair.

The other key adjustment you'll want to make against a tight-passive player is to respect their raises. If a rock suddenly three-bets preflop or raises your bet on the turn, it's almost certain that they're holding a monster. Unless you hold the nuts (or a hand strong enough to justify playing given the odds you're receiving), it's time to back off. Let them have the occasional small pot; you'll beat them the 90% of the time when they're not confident enough to play their hand all the way to showdown.

Tight-Aggressive

Aggressive players are, in general, much more difficult to play against than passive players (which is why we advocate an aggressive style of play throughout this book). However, not all aggressive players are created equal, and there are several different styles that an aggressive player may utilize.

Once upon a time, tight-aggressive (or TAG) play was considered the only style that a serious professional poker player could use. The merits of such play are obvious; you'll generally get your money in with stronger hands, and by pushing your edges aggressively, you'll make the most of your opportunities. You'll generally have a hand that beats the range of hands your weaker opponents are calling your raises with, and by playing aggressively, you both maximize your wins by building pots, and prevent your opponents from seeing free cards.

In fact, a good tight-aggressive style is still the optimal way of beating up on weak opponents like the ones you'll see populating an average $1/$2 table. The style we advocate throughout this book is aggressive and (relatively) tight; it will keep you from making major mistakes while still giving you plenty of opportunities to punish bad opponents.

However, simply playing tightly and aggressively isn't a sure sign that you're playing good poker. While you may see one or two tight-aggressive players at a typical $1/$2 table, they won't all be good players. Some will play much too tight, playing aggressively only with premium hands (which means you can play against these opponents much like you would a tight-passive player); others will play maniacally aggressive with their strong hands, ignoring signs that they might be beaten, thus making them vulnerable to being trapped any time they hold a big hand.

If you do run into a tough tight-aggressive opponent on occasion, don't panic; we'll have some tips later in this book on how to combat tough players. However, if the rest of the table is juicy, and playing against them makes you uncomfortable, it's also perfectly okay to just avoid playing against these opponents as much as possible, and focus instead on easier prey.

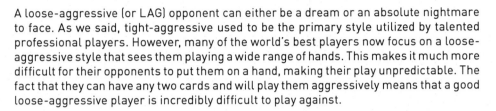

Loose-Aggressive

A loose-aggressive (or LAG) opponent can either be a dream or an absolute nightmare to face. As we said, tight-aggressive used to be the primary style utilized by talented professional players. However, many of the world's best players now focus on a loose-aggressive style that sees them playing a wide range of hands. This makes it much more difficult for their opponents to put them on a hand, making their play unpredictable. The fact that they can have any two cards and will play them aggressively means that a good loose-aggressive player is incredibly difficult to play against.

However, it takes a very high level of poker skill to use a loose-aggressive style. In addition, the style is most effective when you'll be playing against tables that are primarily filled with tight players who can be run over constant aggression. Because a loose-aggressive player will find themselves in many marginal situations with weak hands, it takes a great deal of experience to play this way and not constantly spew money. Though a loose-aggressive style can be used effectively even at the $1/$2 level, it's largely unnecessary; since your primary opponents will be loose-passive players, a loose-aggressive style is more difficult to play (your opponents will often refuse to fold to your aggression) while only offering marginally better profits even if you play this way effectively.

You will occasionally run into loose-aggressive opponents at your tables. But while these players may cause you occasional headaches, don't worry; you'll very rarely be playing against a loose-aggressive pro. Instead, you'll more commonly see players that are best classified as "maniacs" – action players who simply want to play as many hands as possible for as much money as possible. When playing against these players, the key is to get your money in good with a hand that will play well in a big pot. If the money is going on before the flop, that means a big pair or a hand like AK or AQ; if the big action is taking place on the flop or later, you'll want to have made a strong hand (generally a set or better). In contrast to the aggressive style we normally advocate, you'll actually be able to let your maniac opponents lead the action much of the time, as they'll be happy to ship you a large number of chips as long as you continue calling their bets.

Other Player Types

From time to time, we might refer to other types of players. These types generally fit into one of the above categories, but will show some other characteristics that are worthy of note:

- Tricky players will have a tendency to bluff and check-raise. While these weapons are an important part of any player's arsenal, the tricky player will overuse them, often costing themselves bets by attempting a check-raise when simply betting a hand would have won more money, or losing money by making bluffs in situations where they can't possibly work. You'll often be able to identify a tricky player by their tendency to show bluffs, and can often allow exploit their "traps" by inducing bluffs (when out of position) or check-raises (when in position) while holding strong hands.
- Straightforward players will "play their hands face up" by rarely (if ever) bluffing or attempting any of the moves that the tricky player enjoys using. If they bet, they have a hand; if they check, chances are they're weak.
- Players on Tilt are off their game. Maybe they've gotten into a shouting match with an opponent, or maybe they've just had a string of bad beats. In any case, the tilted player is not going to be playing at their best; look for them to make some big mistakes due to anger. If they're having a feud with a specific player at the table, chances are they'll go out of their way to find a way to beat them – even if that means playing fast and loose to get their money in the pot with any two cards.

KEY POINTS

- Your opponents in $1/$2 games will generally be weak, but can fit into many categories.

- The most common type of opponent you'll meet is the loose-passive player: one who calls too frequently with far too many hands.

- Good players almost exclusively play aggressive poker, with both loose-aggressive (LAG) and tight-aggressive (TAG) styles having their merits in different situations.

PART II: PREFLOP PLAY

STARTING HANDS

Before we get into what hands you might want to play, let's first deal with how to evaluate starting hands in a more general sense.

Pairs

Pairs, as you might expect, tend to be pretty strong hands. After all, if you could simply flip over your two cards and declare a hand, even a lowly **22** would beat any unpaired hand!

Of course, Texas Hold'em doesn't quite work that way, so not all pairs are actually very strong hands. The biggest pairs – **AA**, **KK**, and **QQ** – are undoubtedly the three strongest hands in poker, and will often take down pots at showdown even if they don't improve at all. To a lesser extent, this also applies to **JJ**, **TT**, and **99**, all of which should be considered very strong hands.

It may seem intuitively obvious that **KK** is stronger than **TT**. After all, **KK** beats **TT** head-to-head, so it must be stronger! However, there are many more advantages to having a higher pair than simply being able to beat lower pairs. **KK** is significantly stronger than **TT** for several reasons:

- There are more hands – including some fairly strong ones – that **KK** is a substantial favorite over in a showdown situation. For instance, if you should get your money in preflop with **KK** against **QJ**s, you'd have an 82% chance to win; if you hold **TT** against that same hand, you'll basically be in a coin flip situation, with just a 53% chance of winning the hand.
- Higher pairs are much easier to play postflop than lower pairs. On a flop of **Q♥ 9♣ 4♣**, you can be fairly sure that **KK** is likely the best hand. With **TT**, you will also often be best, but it will be much more difficult to fight back against aggression, since that could easily mean a hand like **KQ** made top pair. On the other hand, it could also signal a draw, or a hand like **A9**. With the kings, none of these possibilities is particularly scary (other than a monster draw like **J♣ T♣**), while with tens, it is more difficult for an inexperienced player to figure out if they are way ahead, way behind, or up against a draw.
- Finally, while it doesn't happen often, being on the bad side of a set-over-set situation will usually cost you a lot of money when it does occur. It is significantly more likely for this to occur when you're holding a small pair than a large one, which diminishes their value.

Despite these shortcomings, smaller pairs are still quite valuable. Small and medium pairs – particularly those from **22** up to **88** – derive much of their value from their ability to make a set on the flop. This is especially true for the smallest pairs, while hands like **77** and **88** will occasionally hit flops where, even unimproved, they are very likely to be the best hand. However, most of the value even for these medium pairs comes from the sets they make, as well as the fact that they will often be ahead if you get all-in preflop against a short stack.

Unpaired Hands

Unpaired hands can be evaluated on three different factors: how big the cards in them are, whether or not they are suited, and how connected the two cards are.

The most important of these factors is how high the value of the cards in your hand are. While this is not quite as true in no-limit as it is in limit hold'em, big cards are still significantly more likely to win than smaller ones, all other things being equal. This is especially true in situations where you'll find yourself all-in before the flop; in that case, the ability of your cards to make top pair or win unimproved is critical, so a hand like **A7** is clearly stronger in an all-in situation than **65s**.

Suitedness is also very important to evaluating an unpaired hand. Obviously, suited hands are more likely to make flushes than unsuited hands, which adds some value in a showdown situation. However, the real value to suitedness is that it makes hands much easier to play postflop, as you'll be more likely to flop strong draws that can add value to hands that might otherwise be difficult to evaluate. Since a flush will usually be enough to win a hand (and often a big pot), the ability to make flushes (and flush draws) adds significant value to a hand.

Finally, connected hands are much stronger than unconnected hands, as they are much more likely to make straights using both hole cards. For instance, a hand like **T9** can make a straight that uses both cards in four different ways (anything from a ten-high straight to a king high straight), while a less connected hand like **T7** can only make two different straights that use both cards (either ten-high or jack-high). As with flushes, straights are usually good enough to win fairly large pots, and connected cards also often flop strong draws that will make your hand easier to play.

Put these factors together, and you can probably figure out that the strongest unpaired starting hand would be one that has two high, connected, and suited cards – and you'd be right! **AK**s is the best unpaired hand, and one of the top five or so hands overall (falling somewhere around **JJ** or **TT** in value). Sure, **AKs** can't really take advantage of having connected cards (it can only make one straight, though that one is always the nut straight), but the fact that it contains cards of the two highest values and is suited is enough to put it at the top of the list. Hands like **AK** and **AQs** are also very strong hands, and would likely make most lists of the top 10 starting hands in no-limit hold'em.

Generally, when it comes to unpaired hands, there are a few types of hands we might consider playing – each with their own strengths and weaknesses. Big unsuited cards like **AT** and **KJ** look strong, but will often get into uncomfortable positions post flop. Relatively unlikely to make strong draws, these hands derive most of their value from making top pair with a strong kicker, which is certainly a strong enough hand to win a modest pot – but which will rarely win a large pot.

Those same hands are much stronger when they're suited. A hand like **KQs** is very strong, and has a number of ways to win; the combination of having high card value and the ability to make flushes and straights is enough to make hands like **QTs** strong enough to play in most situations (excluding those where you see significant preflop aggression from your opponents).

Suited connectors are also strong hands, for much of the same reason that small pairs have value – they can make strong hands (in this case, flushes and straights), and it will be difficult for your opponents to figure out what you're holding. When talking about suited connectors, we're mainly talking about hands like **87s** or **54s**; hands with a single gap, like J9s and 86s are also strong. Unsuited connectors like **T9** are significantly weaker than their suited counterparts, but are occasionally playable in some circumstances.

One other hand you'll sometimes like to play is the suited ace-rag, such as **A4s**. These hands take most of their value from their ability to make a nut flush, as well as gaining some extra value due to having an ace. However, don't put too much value in that ace; your weak kicker means you'll often make the second best hand even if you make top pair.

Other hands can be classified as junk, though even here the value of hands can vary wildly. A hand like **K5s** may actually be playable in some rare cases, while **J4** is unlikely to be worth even a limp from the small blind. The problem isn't just that these hands will rarely make the best hand; in addition, they'll also frequently make second-best hands, costing you money frequently even when you "hit" a hand on the flop. The fact that other players in your games will be playing these hands is a big reason why you can turn profits; don't start eating away at your edge by playing these hands as well.

A Basic Starting Hand Solution

It's difficult to make a simple starting hand chart for no-limit hold'em. The truth of the matter is that a proper starting hand strategy has to take into account the styles and ability levels of your opponents, as well as your table image and the sizes of the chip stacks around the table (especially your own).

Of course, saying that isn't going to stop many readers from wanting a starting hand chart! Since it makes sense for new players to have a jumping off point, I've included a chart below that you can use to make most preflop decisions. The chart below isn't perfect for every $1/$2 game, but it should be enough to allow you to turn a profit and put you to as few tough decisions as possible postflop.

As you get more comfortable in your game, and learn more about how to adjust to changing table conditions, you should begin to vary your play. Starting with the guide here, though, should be enough for you to avoid making major mistakes. This guide might even be a tad on the passive side, as it was designed to keep you out of trouble, rather than encourage you to press every small edge. Nonetheless, you will see that the chart will usually have you raising if you're the first player to enter the pot. The reasons behind this will be explained in detail later, but for now, just keep in mind that aggressive play is important to being a winning poker player, and that raising to open the pot gives you a chance to pick up the blinds uncontested.

For the chart below, consider "late position" to be the button or one off the button (also known as the cutoff position). The next two positions closest to the button can be considered "middle position," while anything earlier than that is (you guessed it) "early position." If you see a listing such as **55+**, that means all pairs 55 or higher; similarly, **AT+** means AT and all higher aces.

If Nobody Has Entered the Pot

Early Position: Raise with **TT+, AQ+**, and **KQs**
Call with **22+**, any two suited cards ten or higher, **A2s+, T9s, 98s, 87s, 76s** and **65s**

Middle Position: Raise with **77+, AJ+, KQ** and any two suited cards jack or higher
Call with **22+, A2s+, JTs, T9s, 98s, 97s, 76s, 65s, 54s, QTs, J9s, T8s, 97s, 86s**

Late Position: Raise with **22+, A2s+, T9s, 98s, 87s, 76s, 65s, J9s, T8s, 97s, 86s** and any two cards ten or higher

Small Blind: In practice, if all players fold to the small blind in a $1/$2 no-limit hold'em game, the blinds will almost always agree to "chop" the pot – simply pulling back their blinds and moving on to the next hand. This is due to the fact that the rake will make up a large percentage of the pot (unless the pot grows quite big), and most players will prefer not to contest what they see as an unprofitable situation.

In tournament play, as well as in situations where no rake is taken from the pot (mainly "time charge" games, which are more common at higher buy-ins), playing these situations can be important and profitable. However, in order to keep the table friendly (and, as a consequence, usually looser), simply chopping the blinds in a $1/$2 game is usually the way to go, and I'll recommend that here.

If One or More Players Have Limped (Called) In Front of You

Early Position: Raise with **TT+, AQ+, and KQs**
Call with **22+**, any two suited cards ten or higher, **A2s+, T9s, 98s, 87s, 76s** and **65s**

Middle Position: Raise with **88+, AJ+, KQ** and any two suited cards jack or higher
Call with **22+, A2s+, JTs, T9s, 98s, 97s, 76s, 65s, 54s, QTs, J9s, T8s, 97s, 86s**

Late Position: Raise with **77+** and any two cards ten or higher
Call with **22+, A2s+, J9s, T9s, T8s, 98s, 97s, 87s, 86s, 76s, 75s, 65s, T9** and **98**

Small Blind: Raise with **TT+, AQ+, AJs+, and KQs**
Call with **22-77**, any two cards ten or higher, and any two suited cards

Big Blind: Raise with the same hands you would raise with in the small blind; check with all other hands.

If A Player Has Raised In Front of You

Early Position: Reraise with **QQ+** and **AK**
Call with **66+, AQs, KQs, QJs, and JTs**

Middle Position: Reraise with **JJ+, AQs+, and AK**
Call with **22+, KQs, JQs, JTs, and T9s**

Late Position: Reraise with **TT+, AQs+, KQs, and AQ+**
Call with **22+, KJs, QJs, JTs, T9s, 98s, 87s, 76s, and 65s**

In the Blinds: Use the rules for early position, except call with **22-JJ**.

If There Has Been a Raise and a Reraise

At this point, position will become less important of a factor in most low buy-in no-limit hold'em games; in many cases, it will be apparent that unless someone folds, a player is likely to be all-in either preflop or on the flop. In games where both you and your opponents have very deep stacks (say, over 200 big blinds, or $400 or more in a $1/$2 game), and your opponents are somewhat stronger and more aggressive, you may be able to play these situations similarly to when there has been just a single raise, only tightening up slightly.

However, most $1/$2 games do not fit this description, and thus, most three-bets from your opponents will represent a lot of strength. Certainly, you should be happy to four-bet (often, all-in) with **AA** or **KK**; if the stacks aren't particularly deep, you'll probably want to make this play with at least **QQ** and **AK** as well (and the shorter the remaining effective stacks – meaning, the size of the shorter stack involved in the hand – the wider you can extend this range). With deeper stacks, it will make more sense to occasionally just call a three-bet flat with a lot of hands, including some speculative hands like low pairs and suited connectors. In addition, with deeper stacks, position will once again be a factor; if you will have to act first after the flop, you should be more inclined to want to get the money in preflop with a strong hand, while being in position will afford you more opportunities to see a flop with speculative holdings.

AK in particular deserves a little more discussion here. When it comes to making three-bets or four-bets with **AK**, you'll have to use some discretion. If the money will get all-in preflop, it is usually best to make that reraise with **AK**, thus guaranteeing that you'll see all five cards, ensuring that you have the maximum chance to beat a pocket pair (and that a hand like **AQ** can't bluff you on the flop). However, if you are deep stacked, simply calling a raise with **AK** is fine, and often correct. This will allow you to proceed depending on the texture of the flop, which is typically better than, say, putting $200 in preflop with the hand (at which point you're almost guaranteed to be up against **KK** or **AA**).

We'll examine these topics in greater detail in later chapters. For now, the key takeaway is that a three-bet from most typical $1/$2 opponents signals real strength, and you'll usually need a hand that plays well all-in if you want to stay in the hand.

KEY POINTS

- If you're the player opening the pot, it is nearly always correct to raise rather than limp.

- With sufficiently deep stacks, you can call raises with a wide range of speculative hands (especially in position).

- If opponents are showing strength by three-betting or four-betting, chances are they have a strong hand, and you should only play if you also have a premium holding.

SIZING PREFLOP RAISES

If you've watched the World Series of Poker on television, you've probably noticed that the size of preflop raises has been trending downward in high-level poker tournaments. While 3-4 times the size of the big blind was the common raise sizing just a few years ago, professional players now commonly raise just 2.5 times the big blind, and you'll sometimes even see a min-raise to just twice the big blind late in tournaments.

What does this have to do with how much you should raise in your low-stakes cash game? In practice, not much – though the reason why they raise so little is something we'll get back to in a bit. In most $1/$2 games in casinos, you'll see preflop raises that range from $8 to $12, with raises as high as $15 to $20 (or sometimes even more) being far from rare. That means players are routinely raising to 5-6 times the size of the big blind, with some players choosing to raise as much as 10 times the big blind!

Why are these raises so much larger than those you'll see in tournament play? There are a few reasons why the typical $1/$2 player makes large preflop raises:

- In some casinos, the rake or drop taken from each pot is rather steep in small pots. Players may feel that if they raise to only $5 or $6 and get one caller, too large a percentage of the pot will be going to the casino.
- Many players like to build big pots, and pots tend to grow exponentially based on the size of early bets. Adding a few extra dollars to a preflop raise can lead to a much bigger pot at the end of the hand.
- Many players live in constant fear of seeing their premium holdings beaten by "inferior" hands. They will raise a large amount in an effort to narrow the field, and might even be happy to simply pick up the blinds. Since their opponents call with anything, they're still likely to get at least one call even with an oversized raise.

That final point is a particularly interesting one. Let's make something clear right away: you should not fear playing against weaker hands. Consistently playing against weak players who are willing to put money into the pot with weaker hands than you're holding is an extremely profitable situation. Yes, you'll face some bad beats, but in the long run, the mistakes our opponents make are the only way we can make money – and we should be happy to encourage as many mistakes as possible.

With that in mind, we'd like to make raise sizes that will limit the field somewhat (while playing against nine other players every hand would be profitable, it would also be rather difficult), while still encouraging our opponents who are willing to call our raises with weak holdings to do so.

Let's go back for a moment to the small raises we see in tournament play – especially later in tournaments when the blinds and antes are fairly large compared to the size of the stacks. In these cases, strong players have found that the best strategy is to raise as little as possible while still retaining a fair amount of fold equity, thus giving themselves a good chance of picking up the blinds and antes without a fight. They're not afraid of getting a call from the big blind (who is often getting the chip odds to suggest they should call with any two cards), but picking up just the blinds and antes is a good result. Players are less likely to call in a tournament situation, as calling even a small raise may require committing a significant portion of their stack, and surviving is an important tournament consideration.

In cash games, "survival" has no meaning; if you get stacked, you can always buy more chips and keep playing. As such, players are much more inclined to call a raise – even one that is fairly large. At the same time, simply picking up the blinds isn't a very exciting proposition, so players are unlikely to raise so much as to drive out all potential callers.

When sizing your own preflop raises in a cash game, it's a good idea to keep an eye on the typical raise size at your table. Chances are that you won't want to stray too far outside this range, especially if these raises seem to be doing the job they're meant to do: limiting the field, but still attracting a smattering of calls from loose and passive players.

If you're unsure about how much to raise, starting too low is probably a touch better than starting too high. This is because you're likely to be a superior player postflop compared to most of your opponents; getting a few extra callers and having deeper stacks with which to outplay them is a better result than simply picking up $3 in blinds with a premium hand. Mind you, winning the blinds is not a bad result, by any means; however, if it's happening too often in a typical $1/$2 game, you're likely not maximizing your winning potential.

If you can't judge your raise size based on what you've observed, try starting somewhere in the $7-$8 range. If you are regularly being called by three or more opponents, increase your raises size – you're likely to still get 2-3 calls with a $10-$12 raise, building a similar pot with a better chance to win (thanks to the hands that refused to call for the extra few dollars).

In games against stronger players, these raises would be suicidal; your opponents would exploit the fact that you're raising big by either tightening up and only playing against you with hands that figure to beat your raising range, or by three-betting more frequently to pick up the significant money you've put out there before the flop (or often, some combination of both). However, as long as your opponents aren't making these adjustments, and are instead calling your larger-than-normal raises with weak hands on a regular basis (while rarely three-betting), making raises similar to those you see around the table will simply maximize your edge against your loose opponents.

Adjust to Opponents' Raise Sizing

While your opponents may play badly against large raises, you certainly don't have to. If your opponents are making exceptionally large raises, you should adjust your play in order to take advantage of this.

First, you'll need to identify why your opponents are raising so much. If you're playing against a tight, passive opponent who will only raise with strong hands – and then raises big to protect those hands – there are two possible responses. First, if you have seen the opponent fold to three-bets, you may wish to frequently reraise when they put out a big raise. It's not rare to find a player who will assume every three-bet means AA or KK, and fold anything weaker. Of course, this only works against very tight and skittish players, and also depends on the effective stacks being large enough to induce your opponent to fold. If an opponent raises to $20 and only has another $20 behind, trying to steal the pot is a fool's errand.

On the other hand, you might choose to approach this player more cautiously, particularly if they've shown a willingness to "take a stand" with the few hands they raise with. In that case, simply respect their raises and refuse to play against them with anything but the very best hands. When you do pick up a monster, you can reraise, knowing they're very likely to at least call and play a big pot with you.

Other players will make large raises simply because they're action junkies who enjoy building big pots, but are otherwise the typical loose, passive players who are common at $1/$2 tables. In these cases, you may wish to push your edge by reraising more frequently with strong hands, especially if these reraises are likely to commit you or your opponent to a preflop all-in. The reason is clear: since this opponent is playing big pots with a wide range of hands, and is likely to call your three-bets lightly even when they're committing their stack, you can confidently play large pots against them with hands like **AJ** or **88** and know that you'll show a profit in the long run.

Now, that strategy is high-risk, and does require you to make some inferences about the range of hands your opponent is willing to put money in with. If you're not comfortable playing this way, it's perfectly fine to instead play cautiously against bigger raises, simply tightening up and waiting for big hands like **AA, KK, QQ, JJ, AK** or **AQs** and getting your money in with them. You'll still show a profit this way (though not as large a profit as you would by playing more aggressively), and there is far less risk of making a major mistake.

Against unusually small raises, you should be much more willing to call with speculative hands like small pairs and suited connectors. If small raises are attracting a large number of calls, you may even decide to call with more hands that we'd usually suggest, including some unsuited connectors and many additional suited hands. Don't go crazy with this, however; while **T9** or **75s** may be playable in these situations, **J2s** isn't worth even a minraise against very weak opponents. We'll talk more about why small raises favor these hands in the chapter on stack sizes.

KEY POINTS

- A preflop raise is designed to increase the size of the pot and limit the number of players who see the flop – both of which increase your equity in the hand.

- In $1/$2 live games, the "standard" raise might be anywhere between $6 and $20, depending on your opponents.

- If you're unsure of how much to raise, err low instead of high; it is better to encourage bad hands to call your raises rather than risk your larger raises being exploited by any strong opponents at the table.

STACK SIZES

One of the most important factors in determining how to play a hand is stack size – both the size of your own stack, as well as that of your opponent. But despite the important role played by stack size, it's a topic that most weak players misunderstand at best, and completely ignore at worst.

First of all, it's important to debunk one of the most common misconceptions about stack size. **In a cash game, having a larger stack size does not give you an advantage over your opponents.** That flies in the face of everything most amateur poker players believe, so it deserves an explanation.

It's important to realize that having a larger stack does confer some advantages in *tournament* play. Because survival is important in a tournament situation, having more chips gives you some degree of comfort, as well as the ability to put pressure on smaller stacks who know that playing against you could cost them their tournament lives.

Why doesn't this advantage carry over to live play? Simply put, you can't "eliminate" a player from a cash game. If a player loses when all-in, they can choose to buy more chips and continue playing. Therefore, from a theoretical point of view, there's no advantage to be had simply by having more chips than an opponent.

In fact, there's actually a theoretical advantage to having a very short stack, especially in games that often see several players in a hand – a description that certainly applies to the typical $1/$2 no-limit hold'em game. If a short stack can get all-in early in a hand against multiple opponents with deeper stacks, they have a significant edge, as it's often the case that at least one of those opponents will fold before the river. Those players usually had at least some chance to win the hand, so having them out of the action means that the all-in short stack will win more frequently than if all the players involved made it to showdown. Plus, being guaranteed to see a showdown means that the short-stack can never be bluffed off the hand; a hand like **AK** will often win unimproved, but will rarely stick around to the river without improving unless they get all-in preflop. However, while playing this simplistic short-stacked style is profitable, a good player will make more money by playing with a deeper stack, and that's what we'll focus on throughout this book.

For this theoretical reasoning, you should never feel intimidated by an opponent with a larger stack. However, this whole book is about practical applications, and you will sometimes run into opponents that can be bullied due to their fear of going broke. It's usually easy to identify a player who is terrified of losing their buy-in (a sure sign that they shouldn't be playing in the game in the first place). Against such players, you should adjust to play against them more like you would a scared short-stack on the bubble in a tournament – don't be afraid to put them to decisions for all their chips, because they'll usually fold unless they have the nuts (or close to it).

Adjusting to the Effective Stack Size

In this book, you're going to see the term "effective stack size" used a lot. The effective stack size the amount of money you may be able to play for in a given hand. In a heads-up situation, the effective stack size is equal to the size of the smaller stack. In multiway pots, things get a bit more complex; however, for most applications, it's fine to think of the effective stack size as the size of your stack, or the stack of your opponent that has the most money – whichever is smaller.

For example, imagine you are playing with $200 behind you, and you are in a heads up pot against an opponent that has $1,000 behind. The effective stack size is $200; neither you nor your opponent can lose more than $200. This is actually another reason why having a larger stack doesn't confer any advantage – in the above example, your opponent can really only use his first $200 against you. The remaining $800 can't hurt you unless your opponent decides to throw his chips at you, which is rarely a major concern.

The effective stack size you are playing with is a critical part of determining how you play each hand. When the effective stack size is small – particularly under $60, or 30 times the big blind at a $1/$2 table – you'll want to almost exclusively play hands that play well in all-in situations. This is due to the fact that you'll almost always be all-in by the flop, leaving you little room to maneuver or outplay your opponents. In addition, you won't hit good flops for your speculative hands often enough to justify calling a preflop raise with them; the money you lose when you're forced to fold will far outweigh the money you win when you get all-in with a made set, flush or straight.

With that in mind, hands like **A♥ 9♣** and **K♦ J♠** go up in value when the effective stack sizes are small. These kinds of hands play well when they're all-in early in a hand, as they perform very well heads up against the range of hands most of your opponents will be playing in these situations.

But what about when the effective stack size is very high? You will sometimes find yourself in hands where the players have more than 150 big blinds (over $300 in a $1/$2 game), and these situations are very lucrative – but also very dangerous. The hands we just talked about – big, unpaired, unsuited hands – are great at making top pair hands that will beat lesser hands if they get all-in before the flop. However, they struggle when playing with deep stacks, as they rarely make very strong hands: sets, straights, and flushes. Making top pair, top kicker is great for winning a small pot. On the other hand, if you hold **A♣ K ♥** on a board of:

A♦ T ♣ J♦ 8♦

You'll be in a very tough spot if you bet and then face a large raise from an opponent. In a game with typical loose/passive opponents, you'll often have to fold here, even though you may have the best hand (while against a tight/passive opponent, you can be much more certain that a fold is the right play). Against tough opponents, you'll have to be worried about a bluff – while also knowing that your opponent could easily have you crushed. We'll talk more about this later, but for now, know that keeping the pot relatively small is usually a good idea with these "top pair" hands when you're playing with deep stacks.

However, speculative hands play much better when the effective stack size is high. Hands like **55** or **8♣ 7♣** become very strong when the stacks are deep, especially when playing against weak opponents. While you won't often make the best hand with a small pair or suited connectors, your hand is likely to be well-disguised when you do. Since you'll usually be forced to fold on the flop, you'll need to have the potential of winning a lot of money when you do make a hand – and large stacks give you just that opportunity. Unlike you, many of your opponents are likely to overplay top pair or two pair, giving you the chance to take a lot of chips from them when you make a straight, flush, or set. You can take advantage of this by playing speculative hands that make these hands relatively often, and just waiting for your opportunities to get your money in against overly enthusiastic opponents.

Finally, there are some hands that play well no matter what the effective stack sizes are. Not surprisingly, these are the monster hands, like **AA**, **QQ**, and **A♥ K♥**. Big pairs and big suited connectors will dominate preflop all-in confrontations while also having the potential to win big pots when they improve – as long as you play well after the flop.

KEY POINTS

- Having a bigger stack doesn't give you an advantage over your opponents in a cash game.

- Big unsuited hands do best in situations where the stacks are shallow and the money is likely to go in early in the hand.

- Speculative hands (small pairs, suited connectors) do best with deep stacks, where they can potentially win a lot of money for a small initial investment.

PART III: POSTFLOP PLAY

A POSTFLOP GAMEPLAN

While most of the topics we've discussed so far apply to preflop play, the most difficult decisions in No Limit Texas Hold'em come after the flop. The play on later betting rounds is much more complex, and most poor players have a very weak understanding of proper postflop strategy. This is a double-edged sword; while it means that your opponents may make very costly mistakes on the flop, turn and river, your mistakes will also be magnified. Most of the biggest bets you make during a poker game will take place after the flop, and one wrong move can wipe out the gains from hours of solid play in an instant.

Becoming a true master of postflop play takes a great deal of experience, study, and hard work. However, the focus of this book is to get you to the point where you can win in $1/$2 live games – not to teach you how to fight back against Phil Ivey and Tom Dwan. With that in mind, we're going to lay out a clear and simple game plan that will allow you to take advantage of the most common mistakes your opponents will be making, while steering you away from as many tough decisions and dangerous pitfalls as possible.

The next few chapters will each detail one area of our game plan. First, though, let's give the overall plan a quick overview. Our postflop strategy includes:

*   Value Betting: Against our typical opponents who will frequently call down to the river with relatively weak holdings, we will value bet relentlessly with our strong hands.
*   Continuation Bets: One of the most important weapons in a good poker player's arsenal, we'll frequently throw out continuation bets – especially on the right boards, and against the right opponents.
*   Protecting Hands: While we can't stop our opponents from ever hitting a weak draw, we can at least make chasing those draws unprofitable for them in the long run.
*   Pot Control: Sometimes, we won't want to play a big pot with a marginal hand, but we will want to get to showdown with it. Pot control techniques can help steer our opponents into creating pots that best suit our hands.
*   River Play: The final round of betting is a little different than the previous streets; there are no more draws, only made hands. While a few simple tips can keep you from making the worst river mistakes, you'll be surprised to find just how often your opponents will blunder at the end of hands.
*   Playing Draws: Drawing hands are regularly misplayed by the majority of $1/$2 players. Like other hands, drawing hands should be played aggressively – though that doesn't always mean that you need to take the same line you would with a made hand.
*   Hand Reading: Even at the $1/$2 level, it's important to attempt to put your opponents on ranges and adjust your strategy accordingly. While hand reading is as much an art as a science, there are some basic tips you can use to begin to narrow down your opponents' holdings.

We'll be talking about plenty of other topics in these chapters, and once you're done reading, you should feel confident about having a significant postflop edge against the vast majority of your $1/$2 opponents.

VALUE BETTING

The most basic, straightforward and common bet you'll make in No Limit Texas Hold'em is the value bet. Simply put, a value bet is a bet that's made when you expect to be called by a hand that is likely worse than your hand. You don't have to be entirely certain that your hand is best in order to make a value bet; you only need to believe that, in the long run, you will get called by inferior hands the majority of the time.

In much of poker literature, the term value bet is only used in situations where the author is talking about a thin value bet – one in which the decision is close, and in which you'll be betting a marginal hand after carefully considering your opponent's range of possible hands. This is for good reason, because even bad players understand that you should generally bet with your very strong hands, but often miss the value that they can get from marginal-to-strong hands. That said, it's important to understand that on a basic level, even betting with the nuts is a type of value bet, since the goal is to get called – thus getting "value" for your hand.

Here's an example of a typical (and fairly easy to make) value bet:

With a stack of **$200***, you hold* **A♥ Q♣** *on the button. Two players limp in front of you. You raise to* **$10***, and are called by both limpers. There is* **$33** *in the pot. The flop comes:*

3♥ 8♣ Q♠

Both limpers check to you. What do you choose to do?

The obvious answer is to make a value bet – probably somewhere in the range of $15-$25. You are almost guaranteed to have the best hand here, but there are a number of hands that your typical opponents in a $1/$2 game will be happy to call down with. Among some of the hands that a loose-passive player is likely to have here, you can expect calls from any queen, any eight, hands like **A3, T9, JT, J9** and small pocket pairs. Will an opponent occasionally have **QQ, 88, 33,** or **Q8**? Sure, that'll happen. But since there is a much better chance that at least one of your opponents will have a hand that they want to call with than one that has you beat, you'd be losing a lot of value by not betting here.

Okay, that example was extremely simple – even a very tight, very passive is likely to make a bet with top pair, top kicker. Here's an example that may better illustrate how most players miss value bets during play:

With effective stacks at **$200***, you hold* **Q♠ T♥** *in middle position. One player limps in early position, and you decide to limp behind them; another player limps behind you. The big blind checks, and four players head to the flop with a* **$9** *pot. The flop comes down:*

K♣ 8♠ 5♦

The big blind checks, as does the player in early position. You choose to check, and the player in late position checks behind. The turn is a **T♦***. The action is checked to you again. What should you do?*

This is an excellent spot to bet with your hand. You hold second pair with a good kicker, and nobody has yet shown any willingness to bet out at the pot. Most of your opponents could easily have any two cards here. A bet of $6 or so will often take down the pot right here, but you're not on a bluff – in fact, if you get called, you'll still often have the best hand. In most games, you'll be called here by any king, any ten, and a lot of eights and fives as well. There are also a number of straight and flush draws that are likely to call your bet despite the fact that they're not getting the odds to do so. Only a king, AT, two pair, or a set has you beat here, and it's likely that an opponent with one of those hands would have bet at this point. A value bet here will make you money in the long run.

This example illustrates an important rule about value betting: you can't be scared simply by the presence of overcards on the board. Betting second pair with a good kicker is the kind of aggressive play that's necessary to beat $1/$2 no limit games.

When Not to Value Bet

Generally, we don't want to risk a value bet when our hand has a small amount of value, but can't beat anything other than a bluff. There may be times when a bet with such a hand is profitable, but it certainly isn't because we're betting for value. For example, on a board of:

3♣ K♦ 9♠ 6 ♣

It's possible that a hand like **A♥ 3♥** is best here – but there's no sense in betting for value. No hand that we have beat (with the exception of some draws) will ever call us here, while any king, nine or six has us beat. If you have the chance to check and see the river for free, it's probably worth taking that opportunity; After all, should an ace or three come on the river (with the possible exception of the **A♣**, which could complete a flush), you'll likely have the best hand.

Another time to avoid betting for value is when you make a monster, and it's unlikely that any of your opponents could have possibly hit the board – but you suspect that giving them a free card might help them catch up just enough to get themselves into trouble. For instance, if you hold **J♥ J♦** and the flop comes:

J♣ J♠ 2♠

You've flopped the nuts, but a bet here may not be prudent. Nothing much is left on the board to help your opponents, unless you're lucky enough for one of them to have been holding pocket deuces. On the other hand, if a spade or an ace hits on the turn, there's a good chance that one of your opponents may make a flush or top pair. In addition, your refusal to bet the flop may make an opponent with a hand like **TT** or **99** more confident in their hand; they may surmise that a hand like **QQ** or higher would have bet the flop, so you could easily have **AK** or **AQ**. Of course, if we did have any of those hands, we would have bet the flop nearly 100% of the time – but that's a topic for the next chapter.

Value betting is a very complex topic, and we'll touch on it a lot throughout the rest of the book. In order to take full advantage of value bets, you'll need to take many factors into consideration, including board texture and the possible range of hands your opponents may hold. For now, the key thing to grasp is that betting when **you have the best hand and are getting calls** is the surest way to make money against weaker poker players – the occasional bad beats you suffer are more than made up for by the times they don't make their hands.

KEY POINTS

- Value bets are bets made when you expect to be called by an inferior hand.

- Value bets are especially strong against opponents who rarely fold; even second pair with a good kicker will often be ahead of such an opponent's range.

- Getting calls from weaker hands is a good thing – in fact, it's the primary you'll make money from poker!

CONTINUATION BETS

If you've watched televised poker in the last few years, or even talked about poker with anyone who has more than a small amount of experience playing the game, you're probably familiar with the term **continuation bet**. A continuation bet is a bet made on the flop by the preflop raiser. The name comes from the fact that these bets are a continuation of the aggression shown by the raiser preflop. Since the raiser took control of the hand before the flop, it makes sense that they'll usually have an opportunity to take the initiative on the flop as well.

The continuation bet is an extraordinarily powerful weapon in the hands of an aggressive player. During the poker boom that started after Chris Moneymaker's victory in the 2003 World Series of Poker, an aggressive style of tournament poker began to dominate over the classical, conservative style that had ruled tournament play for the previous three decades.

While television audience marveled at how players like Gus Hansen could win by playing nearly any two cards in any position, many players missed the biggest factor in the dominance of these aggressive players: their ability to pick up an enormous number of small pots simply by making continuation bets. In fact, it wasn't unheard of for some players to make continuation bets 100% of the time, regardless of their opponents' tendencies or the texture of the flop! Almost universally, players would fold often enough to make these plays very profitable, allowing aggressive players to build chip stacks with very little risk. While continuation bets have become more refined in recent years, frequent "c-bets" are still an important part of any good player's arsenal.

In a $1/$2 cash game, there's one major factor that works against the continuation bet: the fact that many of your opponents will fit the loose-passive mold meaning they already fold less often than they should. However, that's far from saying that you should abandon the continuation bet entirely. In fact, making smart continuation bets is a big part of a winning $1/$2 strategy.

The Basic Continuation Bet

As we said earlier, the basic idea behind the continuation bet is simple. If you raised preflop and get called by one or more players, and the action comes around to you without anyone having made a bet, simply make a bet of around half the size of the pot (or slightly more – you'll generally want to make all of your different kinds of bets for a similar size, to ensure that you don't give tells based on bet sizing). If you take down the pot about one-third of the time, you'll break even; since, under the right conditions, you should expect to take down the pot right here over half the time, these continuation bets will show a tremendous profit for you.

Here's an example of the continuation bet in action:

A player limps in early position. You raise to $8 from middle position with K♣ Q♥. All other players fold to the original limper, who calls, making the pot $19. The flop comes:

9♦ 2♣ 6♠

The player in early position checks. You make a continuation bet of $10, and your opponent folds.

When making your continuation bets, remember that it does not matter what your hand is – you'll be making the same kind of bet whether you hit the flop or not. Thus, it is impossible for your opponents to distinguish your "bluff" continuation bets from the bets you're making for value.

The key to the continuation bet actually lies in your opponents' hands. A given unpaired hand will only hit the flop approximately one-third of the time. The other two-thirds of the time, it will be very difficult for your opponents to call a bet. This is even true for the loose-passive opponents we've talked about throughout this book; while they may be more likely to call, they're still unlikely to stay in a hand if they've missed completely.

Also, understand that your continuation bet does not mean that you have to continue putting bets into the pot on future streets if your opponent makes the call on the flop. If you have nothing, and you don't improve on the turn, it's perfectly okay to give up. If you're in position, chances are that the action will get checked to you on the turn as well; if you haven't made a hand worth betting at that point, you can always check and take a free card on the river. That's another advantage of the continuation bet – even when your opponents stick around in the hand, they may often give you the opportunity to make a hand on a later street by letting you keep the initiative for another betting round.

When to Make Continuation Bets

Some situations are better for continuation bets than others. A few factors that should swing you in the direction of making continuation bets are the following:

Weak/Tight Opponents: If you're in a hand with an opponent who folds far too often (particularly a tight-passive player, but sometimes tight-aggressive players as well), it is likely correct to make continuation bets 100% of the time. Okay, it's true that even the least observant opponents are likely to eventually notice what you're doing, so it might be right to skip the occasional c-bet in the worst situations (we'll outline some of those for you below). But most of these players will simply grit their teeth, complain quietly (or not so quietly) about those darn Internet kids and their wild play, and wait until they finally have a hand to trap you with – not realizing that you're making way more money on the hands you win than you'll lose the one time they spring their "trap."

Favorable Board Textures: Not all flops are created equal. One of the advances in continuation bet theory over the last decade has been the idea that there are certain boards that favor continuation bets, and others that probably aren't profitable. Essentially, this is based on how likely it is that your opponent hit the board and made a hand (or a strong draw). Some of the best flops are as follows:

- Paired Boards: Any board including a pair is highly unlikely to have helped a single opponent. Examples include **7♥ 7♠ 3♣** and **T♣ T♠ 5♠**.
- Dry Boards: A dry board is one that doesn't contain many possible draws, meaning it's unlikely that your opponent is on a strong flush or straight draw. For instance, **4♥ A♣ 8♠** and **K♣ 2♦ 4♥** would both be considered dry boards.

You've Hit the Board: Of course, any time you hit the board in any way, you should strongly consider making a continuation bet. Since you want to be making these bets very often, it makes more sense to skip the continuation bet occasionally when you miss rather than miss a bet when you've made a hand. The main exception to this comes when you make a monster and you believe your opponents all likely missed the board; you might check through then to give your opponents a chance to improve.

However, even hitting the board weakly should usually be enough to throw out a continuation bet. With a flush, straight, or combination draw, you might even be able to take advantage of the situation we mentioned earlier in this chapter, and get to see both the turn and river for the price of a single bet.

When Not to Make Continuation Bets

There are a few situations in which you may choose not to make continuation bets on a regular basis, and instead only bet the flop if you have a hand you can bet for value. The most common factors that would point you in this direction are:

You're Facing an Opponent Who Won't Fold: We all know the type – some opponents simply refuse to fold. Again, this doesn't mean the typical loose-passive player who doesn't fold quite often enough; we're talking about players who will call down with any two cards unless you bet an absurd amount on the flop. You'll win your money from these players by value betting again and again; making continuation bets against them when you don't have a hand is just throwing away money.

You're Facing Multiple Opponents: The more opponents that are in a hand, the less likely it is that they've all missed the flop. With two opponents, continuation bets are still a good idea on very favorable boards, even if you've missed the flop entirely yourself. With three or more opponents, it is probably best to skip continuation bets, and focus instead on making value bets when you have a hand that's worth betting.

Unfavorable Board Textures: Some flops are relatively likely to have hit an opponent who called your preflop raise. The range of a player who will call your preflop raise but not raise or reraise themselves is very rich in queens, jacks and tens. This is less true when dealing with loose-passive opponents who will call with a wide range of hands; however, unless your opponent is so loose that they have virtually no starting hand requirements, it's likely that hands like **QT, JT, Q9, KQ, KJ** and others make up a significant part of their range. With that in mind, it's often a good idea to skip making continuation bets on boards that feature a lot of these cards, such as **Q♣ T♥ 7♠**.

There's a corollary to this that's important to remember: boards with aces and kings are a lot more likely to have hit the preflop raiser's hand than a caller's hand. This is especially true when an ace hits the flop and you're playing an opponent who thinks about the game – but only a little bit. These players have a habit of trying to put other players on a single hand, and if you raise preflop, that single hand is often **AK**. Of course, you won't always hit the flop when you raise and an ace hits, but if your opponents are always going to put you on an ace, you may as well bet out when one hits and take down the pot.

You'll also want to be cautious on wet boards – those flops that feature a lot of potential draws. This is actually a concept that goes well beyond how to play the flop; wet boards are always significantly more dangerous than dry boards, particularly when you hold a vulnerable hand like top pair.

A great example of a wet board is **T♣ 8♣ Q♥**. Not only is there a potentially made straight on the board (should your opponent have J9), but there are plenty of other straight draws available, along with a flush draw for anyone holding two clubs. Combine that with the fact that another player may have hit a queen or a ten, and this is a situation in which a continuation bet may be less attractive.

In addition, if you hit this flop with a hand like **AQ** (without the flush draw), your hand may be best – but it's also very vulnerable. With that in mind, when you do choose to make continuation bets on wet boards, you'll want to make them larger than you normally would – perhaps two-thirds to three-quarters of the size of the pot. This will discourage players from chasing their draws; if they do, you'll likely be setting a price that makes it a mistake for all but the strongest draws to call (we'll talk more about this in the chapter on protecting hands).

If you yourself should have flopped a strong draw (or made a straight or flush), you can still make the larger-than-average continuation bet; your opponents will likely think you're just protecting your hand, as usual. Alternately, if your opponents are particularly unobservant and you've flopped an extremely strong hand (such as the nut flush or straight), you can try making a smaller continuation bet again, encouraging your opponents to stay in with weaker draws. If they should be "lucky" enough to hit their hand, you may take them for their entire stack.

Keep in mind that just because you choose not to make a continuation bet on the flop, that doesn't mean that you can't make a continuation bet later on. If you see a board that's not good for a continuation bet and the hand gets checked through, strongly consider making a **delayed continuation** bet on the turn if the action gets back to you without anyone else having made a bet. If nobody is willing to stab on the turn (or behind you on the flop), it's likely that they're willing to give up – you'll just have to make a bet so that they get the chance to fold.

KEY POINTS

- A continuation bet is a bet made by the preflop raiser on the flop.

- Continuation bets can be made whether you hit the flop or not.

- Some flops are bad for continuation bets, particularly "wet" boards that contain several potential draws.

PROTECTING HANDS

The single biggest complaint most players have about playing $1/$2 No Limit Texas Hold'em (or in small stakes limit games, for that matter) is that their opponents suck out on them too often. They believe that if their opponents would just play "the right way" and not chase weak draws, they'd have much better results.

Of course, nothing could be further from the truth. As we've talked about earlier, we want players calling us with weak hands, including weak draws. In the long run, these plays only serve to make us money, and we should welcome them at every opportunity. Some suck outs simply come with the territory.

On the other hand, there are times when many players – especially loose-passive players – will invite suckouts that could have been avoided. These players often fail to protect their vulnerable hands, then turn around and complain when other players beat them on later streets!

What qualifies as a vulnerable hand? Essentially, any hand that is not strong enough to win should a likely drawing hand improve is a vulnerable hand – particularly if that hand doesn't have a good chance to improve itself. In no-limit hold'em, that will include one pair hands, and will often include two pair, trips, and sets as well. Even a made straight can be vulnerable in a number of cases.

One mistake commonly made by novice poker players is to slowplay hands that should be bet aggressively. Take, for instance, a hand like **A♠ T♥** on a board of **T♦ 8♠ 5♦**. It is likely that this is the best hand here, but it is an extremely vulnerable hand. Any player with two diamonds has a flush draw, while there are a ton of straight draws: **76**, **97**, and **J9** all have open-ended straight draws.

It is essential that a hand like **AT** bets here to protect their hand. In fact, not making a bet here is a critical mistake not only because it may allow other players a free shot to catch up, but for at least two other important reasons as well:

- If a blank comes on the turn, you're less likely to get action if you have the best hand. While weak players do chase draws, even the worst players usually realize that they're less likely to hit their draw with just one more card to come rather than two – and will have less time to capitalize on hitting those draws, as well.
- If any diamond, queen, jack, nine, seven, or six comes on the turn, you will be put in a spot where it is much more difficult to bet, as all of those cards complete

draws. Even the remaining eights and fives could improve another player to trips. While you can still make a bet here to try to take the pot down, players may call with both draws and made hands, attempting to trap you (against most opponents in $1/$2 games, you can safely fold to a raise here – they'll rarely be bluffing). If another player bets, it will be extremely hard for you to call, knowing you'll be facing a river card that could improve your opponent's hand and another round of betting.

How do we protect our vulnerable hands? In limit poker, this is a tricky topic, as a single bet may often still leave our opponents in a position where calling is profitable for them. However, no-limit makes it fairly simple to protect our hands: we simply make a bet that makes it unprofitable for our opponents to call. Generally, we can make the same kind of bet sizes that we would make for a continuation bet, trending towards the higher end of that range on wet boards. Remember, it's important not to change your bet size based on the strength of your hand, as even weak opponents may pick up on this (and stronger players certainly will); on the other hand, adjusting to the board texture is perfectly fine, and shouldn't give away anything about your own hand.

This betting size should be sufficient to prevent all but the strongest draws from getting the proper odds to call your bets. In situations where neither you nor your opponents will be all-in, the odds of your opponent completing their draw on the next card are more important than their overall odds of completing. This is due to the fact that you can force them to call another bet on the turn should they miss their draw initially.

While we've promised to stay light on the math throughout this book, this is one of those spots where it's helpful to know a few important numbers. Let's look at the hand from your opponent's perspective. So far, they know five cards – the two in their hand, and the three on the flop. If they hold a flush draw (with, say, **A♦ 2♦** in our example), they have nine outs to complete the draw. That means they have about a 19% chance of making their draw, and would require a little better than 4-1 in immediate pot odds in order to make their call profitable. A straight draw **(J♠ 9♥)** would have eight outs to improve to a straight (we'll ignore the fact that a diamond that completed their draw might scare them, as it would also make a flush). This gives them a 17% chance of completing their draw on the next card, meaning they'll need nearly 5-1 odds in order to have an immediately profitable call.

Of course, the implied odds these hands have make them significantly stronger than these odds would suggest. However, if you make a bet of two-thirds of the pot, you'll be laying only 2.5-1 pot odds. As long as you play well for the rest of the hand, you will not pay your opponents off nearly enough to make these calls profitable. Of course, if they fold to your bet, that's fine too; you'll have taken down a pot without having to contend with an opponent who had a fairly good chance of winning the pot at showdown.

Of course, there are some draws that are so strong that you'll never get them to fold. For instance, a player holding **J♦ 9♦** has an open-ended straight flush draw, and actually has about a 63% chance of beating your hand by showdown! However, the possibility of these kinds of draws should not be enough to stop you from protecting your hands. In fact, if your opponents play these draws passively – as many opponents will do, afraid to put money into the pot without a made hand – this situation is only slightly profitable for them (remember, they're a favorite overall, but not to complete on the next card), and the fact that you've made them pay to see each card is still better for you than simply allowing them to see those cards for free.

If a Player May Move All-In

Stack size can play an important role in determining how best to protect your hand. While the rules above work well when stacks are deep, short stacks can significantly impact how you evaluate these situations.

Since an all-in situation guarantees a showdown, our rule about only considering the odds that a draw will complete on the next card goes out the window. Instead, we're now concerned about the likelihood that a draw will complete by the end of the hand. For a flush draw, you can expect the hand to complete nearly 40% of the time against top pair (remember, they could hit runner-runner to two pair or trips); an-open ended straight draw will be closer to 35%. In either case, a player getting 2-1 odds is correct to call an all-in bet, knowing they'll make their hand often enough to show a profit in the long run.

Despite these improved odds, it is still often possible to protect your hand against likely draws. For instance, if there is $20 in the pot, and your sole opponent has $40 left, the best you can do is put him all in. There will then be $60 in the pot, and it will cost him $40 to call. Those are odds of 3-2 – not enough for a weak draw to profitably call (though enough for a hand such as a flush draw and an overcard to sometimes show a slight profit against a top pair hand).

This illustrates an important point – when the stacks are short and you have a made hand, moving all-in is often your best play. Doing so maximizes your fold equity by putting as much pressure on your opponent as possible without giving them a chance to improve their hand. If you're playing with an effective stack of twice the current pot or less on the flop, and you hold a vulnerable hand, it's likely best to just get your money in at that point. Yes, sometimes you'll get called by a bigger hand and lose, but more often, you'll get hands that could have caused you trouble to fold – or call you with insufficient odds to make that play profitable.

Even if you don't have enough money in front of you to truly "protect" your hand, it's best to force your opponent on a draw to put money into the pot – even if it is mathematically correct to call. If you're ahead in the hand, every dollar that goes into the pot makes the hand more profitable for you. Your opponent may be right to make the call, but they'd much rather see the remaining cards for free rather than have to pay for them. They're actually losing money on the call itself; the drawing hand remains profitable only because of the money that was already in the pot.

KEY POINTS

- If you have a vulnerable hand that is likely best now, it's almost always correct to make a bet.

- When you protect your hand, you make money in the long run whether your opponents fold (giving you the pot) or call while not receiving the proper odds.

- With shorter stacks, sometimes moving all-in is the best way to protect your hand; this move offers you the most fold equity, reduces the pot odds you are giving your opponent, and eliminate implied odds as a consideration.

POT CONTROL

If we could have our way all the time, we'd always get our opponents to put their stacks in the pot when we held the nuts. Meanwhile, when we held decent but marginal hands, our opponents would be courteous enough to allow us to get to a cheap showdown without putting us to a test for most of our chips.

Alas, our opponents aren't always so kind; after all, they have their own ideas about how each hand should play out. That said, there are a number of ways we can influence pot size in order to try to get the types of pots we want for the types of hands we have.

Creating a Big Pot

The simple rule of thumb is "big hands for big pots." If you're playing in a tough game with professional players, you won't always be able to stick to this rule; you're going to have to mix up your play and occasionally run big bluffs to keep your opponents guessing. But if you're playing $1/$2, there's rarely a reason to make big bluffs – both because you won't need to worry about balancing your play as much (for the most part, your opponents aren't going to be keeping track of your tendencies), and also because they're less likely to work against passive players who are apt to all you down. Instead, if you're going to be playing a big pot – one in which you'll be putting big bets in on every street, or moving all-in with a large stack on an early street – you should do so when you feel confident that you have the best hand.

Sometimes, these hands will play themselves, and you'll get all the money in fast. This commonly occurs with big preflop confrontations like AA vs. KK, or in situations where both players flop sets. But more commonly, you'll find yourself in a situation similar to the follow example:

You raise to **$10** *in middle position with* **7♠ 7♦**. *One player calls in late position; all others fold. The flop comes:*

7♥ A♣ Q♠

The pot size is **$23**, *and your remaining effective stack is* **$200**. *How do you proceed?*

You've hit just about the perfect flop for your hand – one in which you've not only made a set, but which your opponent is fairly likely to have hit. Sometimes, your opponents will have had a hand like **TT**, and may fold to your flop bet (or call once before giving up). But your goal here should be to get a hand like **AQ** or **AK** to potentially put in their entire stack by the river, not worry about squeezing a few extra dollars out of a marginal hand that will never call off a significant amount of money.

In this case, it's likely that you'll have to get bets in on every street in order to have a chance to win the other player's entire stack. It's possible that your opponent may help you out by raising. However, you should plan to bet all three streets yourself; if your opponent helps you out, so much the better.

In order to get all of our money in by the river, we'll need to make some relatively big bets. However, since we're acting on the assumption that our opponent has made a strong hand themselves, then our opponent will likely be happy to call these bets. With another $200 to put in the pot, one way to get all the money in would be as follows:

- On the flop, bet $20 into a pot of $23; if called, the new pot is $63.
- On the turn, bet $50 into a pot of $63; if called, the new pot is $163.
- On the river, bet the remaining $130.

Of course, this plan could be adjusted slightly if you believe that your opponent is willing to call off more money early in the hand, but would be scared of a relatively large river bet even with a hand as good as two pair. The key is to make sure that all of your bets are reasonable, while still maximizing the amount of money you can get from a strong hand.

Try not to make ridiculously oversized bets, even if it's possible that an opponent with the perfect second-best hand might call them. For one, it will likely become obvious – even to weak opponents – that you are only doing this with your monster hands. Secondly, while we do want to structure out bets to get the most out of strong hands, we would like to get one or two of our bets called even by slightly weaker hands, if possible. In our example above, a typical loose-passive opponent is likely to call our $20 bet with hands like **AT**, **KQ**, and **QJ**; in some cases, opponents with hands like **AJ** and **AT** could even call the $50 on the turn unimproved. In nearly all cases, playing the hand this way will tend to get the most out of our opponents.

In other cases, we may be able to expect our opponent to fire a continuation bet on the flop, or we may have a stack size and pot size that realistically allow us to get the money in over the course of just one or two bets. The key is to have a plan that will give you a blueprint to maximize your wins with big hands. If something happens that requires you to change that plan, that's fine – you can always make adjustments.

Keeping the Pot Small

When most players discuss pot control, they tend to focus on how to keep pots small when they have a hand that isn't very strong. However, it's important not to get carried away with this idea. While there are certainly times in which controlling the size of the pot to keep it small is beneficial, there are many other instances where "pot control" is used as justification for being scared of playing aggressively, and actually costs players bets.

Going out of your way to keep the pot small is best done with medium-strength hands that will sometimes win at showdown, but aren't strong enough to call large bets. For instance, take the following example:

You raise to $8 from middle position with 7♠ 7♥. All fold to the big blind, who quickly calls. The flop comes:

A♠ J♣ 5♦

The pot is now $17. The big blind checks to you, and you make your standard continuation bet of $10. The big blind once again calls, making the pot $37. The turn is the 4♦. The big blind checks to you again. How should you proceed?

Many loose-passive opponents will refuse to lead out with a bet against a preflop aggressor if they haven't made at least top pair with a strong kicker, so your opponent could be calling you with a wide range of hands. While he might be occasionally calling with a lower pocket pair or a weak straight draw, it's more likely that he holds an ace or a hand like **QJ**, **KJ**, **JT** or **J9**. We are well behind the range of our opponent, but not so far behind that our hand is hopeless; we might expect to show up with the best hand at showdown somewhere around 20-30% of the time, depending on our opponent.

There are two ways you could play here in hopes of keeping the pot small and seeing a cheap showdown. The first, and most straightforward, is just to check back the turn. The problem here is that even a weak opponent is likely to read your continuation bet followed by a check behind on the turn as weakness, inviting them to bet with a wide variety of hands on the river. While you might beat a small part of the range they choose to bet with in that case (or get bailed out if a seven hits on the river), and you will probably have to call a small bet, you'll usually be beaten. The upside to this method is that your opponent may still check the river if they're not happy about their hand; occasionally, you'll save a bet when they have a weak jack and simply weren't confident enough to make a bet.

The alternative method is to make a blocking bet on the turn, with the idea of likely getting your opponent to check to you on the river. A bet of half the pot or less may accomplish one of several things for you:

- If your opponent has a weak hand, they may fold, giving you the pot. This is a great outcome for you in the case of "weak" draws like gutshot straights with what your opponent does not realize are overcards to your sevens. A tight-passive opponent may even fold a lot of jacks to this bet, though you shouldn't count on this happening very often.
- If your opponent has what they consider a marginal hand, they may call, then plan to check to you on the river. That will allow you to get to the showdown for only the price of your turn bet; you'll occasionally even win at showdown against busted draws or lower pairs.
- If your opponent has a strong hand, they may raise you here, after which you can safely fold. Similarly, an opponent who calls the turn and then leads out on the river is also showing great strength; if you don't improve on the river, you can fold in this situation as well.

On rare occasions, you'll lose your small turn bet this way when you could have seen a showdown for free (those times when your opponent has you beat, but wouldn't have bet the river if you checked behind on the turn). However, this will usually more than be made up for by the times you win the pot with your turn bet, along with the dollars you save by making a turn bet that's smaller than the river bet your opponent likely would have made.

The above example is not a general guide on how to keep the pot small; rather, it should serve to illustrate the kinds of things you'll want to think about when planning to control the size of the pot. In some cases, that may mean checking and hoping your passive opponents will stay that way; in other cases, it may mean showing aggression with a small bet in order to keep your opponents from getting aggressive on the next street. It's also worth noting that pot control is much more difficult to maintain when you are out of position; since your opponent now has the option of ending the betting round or making a bet/raise, you won't be able to close out the betting with a check.

Most importantly, try not to get in the habit of thinking about keeping the pot small too often. If you hand is good enough to continue on with, it's usually good enough to bet; if your hand is so weak that it's extremely unlikely to win at showdown, it may be better to just give up and go into check/fold mode rather than put any more money into the pot at all. Pot control techniques are best used sparingly, in specific situations, and against opponents who are likely to cooperate. If you're not sure whether to keep the pot small or continue playing the hand as normal, it's best to err on the side of making standard bets for value.

KEY POINTS

- When you have a monster hand, and your opponent could reasonably have a strong hand themselves, plan to make bets that will allow you to get the entire effective stack into the pot by the river, if possible.
- If you want to keep a pot as small as possible, you might need to think outside the box; sometimes a bet now can save you money on a later street.
- Pot control techniques should be used sparingly; if you're unsure, play a hand aggressively rather than worrying about keeping the pot small.

RIVER PLAY

River play may seem relatively simple. After all, you finally know your hand, and you only have one betting round left before you get to showdown. There are no more draws to worry about, since there are no cards left to come.

However, there are other considerations at play that make river play both difficult and consequential. In no-limit games, the pot grows exponentially, so river bets tend to be bigger than those made on earlier rounds. That makes each mistake costlier – making a bad call can cost you a significant portion of your stack, and folding the winning hand can cost you a monster pot.

While there's a lot that can be said about playing the river properly, our goal as always is to keep things relatively simple for you, rather than overloading you with theoretical concepts that simply won't be relevant in most $1/$2 games. However, there is a golden rule of playing the river that should always be followed:

If a river bet won't be called by a weaker hand, and won't cause a superior hand to fold, it is never worth making.

It's a simple concept, but one that the players in your live casino games will routinely violate, spewing chips in cases where their bets make no sense whatsoever. Essentially, this rule creates three classes of hands:

- Strong hands that we can bet for value, as they will be called by a significant number of hands that are worse.
- Marginal hands that we can't bet for value, but with which we would like to see a showdown.
- Weak hands that have no showdown value, but with which we might occasionally like to bluff.

The exact size of each of these ranges is heavily dependent on our opponents. However, if you're playing against typical loose-passive players, the following guidelines are generally worth following:

- Your value betting range should be fairly wide, as your opponents are likely to call with relatively weak hands. For instance, top pair is probably worth a value bet on most boards that don't contain a high number of likely draws.
- Bluffs should be used sparingly, and only against players who have a tendency to fold too often. If your opponent is a calling station, most bluffs will only cost you money in the long run.

Most players have little trouble playing their strong hands (of course, they bet) or their very weak hands (other than perhaps bluffing too often). Marginal hands, as always, are the most difficult to play. Let's look at an example of a common river mistake:

You hold 7♥ 6♥ out of position against one opponent. The river has just been dealt, and the board reads:

3♣ 6♠ J♥ 8♥ 3♦

The pot is $30, and it is your turn to act. What should you do?

You have third pair on a board where many draws (including some of your own) have missed. It is quite possible that your opponent has a missed draw, though they may also have passively played a jack, an eight, or a higher pocket pair. Your hand has some showdown value, but not much.

A common mistake here is to make a bet of around $15-$20. What could such a bet possibly accomplish? A missed draw is going to fold here, while any hand that has you beat will at least call, if not raise. It's possible you might get a call from a hand like **44**, but that's about it. If you have the best hand, your bet will almost never gain you anything; if you have the worst hand, you'll simply be handing your opponent money.

Instead, imagine what might happen should you check. Depending on your opponent, the outcome may differ, but in all cases, your outcome will be better than by betting:

- A passive opponent will likely check behind, giving you a free showdown that you may well win. They will rarely bluff the river; if they make a bet, you can feel fairly confident that they have you beat.
- An aggressive opponent will often check behind with their own marginal hands, giving you a free showdown. If they bet, they will bet with a range that includes many bluffs; while your hand won't usually be best, you can call a normal sized bet and feel confident that you'll win often enough to show a profit. If your opponent makes an oversized bet, you can fold – but most of the time, calling against a tough (or maniacally aggressive) opponent will be correct. At worst, it is no worse than making a bet in the first place.

The problem with betting a marginal hand in this spot is that you turn a hand with some showdown value into a complete bluff. Since you may be able to win at showdown, why lose that value by making a bet that gains you nothing? Instead, if you want to bluff (a perfectly reasonable thing to do occasionally against tough opponents, as well as tight-passive opponents who fold far too often), do it with a hand that otherwise has no value whatsoever.

In fact, if you're out of position on the river, it's often a good idea to check even with hands you'd normally bet for value – if you believe your opponent is unlikely to call a bet from you, but will often bluff at the pot if you check the river. This is known as **inducing a bluff**, and is one way to combat some of your trickier or more aggressive opponents. Against the typical loose-passive opponent, betting with a value hand is almost always the way to go; however, against habitual bluffers, inducing bluffs when out of position will earn you a lot of extra river bets that you normally wouldn't be able to get out of your opponents.

Sizing River Bets

As a default, it's fine to stick to our normal betting size on the river – perhaps trending to the lower end of that range, since we're already dealing with larger betting amounts, and we do not have to protect our hands against any potential draws. That would make the average river bet around 50-60% of the size of the pot. If you're unsure about how to size your river bets, you'll rarely make any huge mistakes by betting this amount.

That said, there are ways to manipulate the size of our bets in order to get more value on the river. Even against the weakest opponents, there is some correlation between the size of our bets on the river and how often we will get called. As we've discussed earlier, we don't want to vary the size of our bets based on the strength of our own hands, as that would give away too much information to our opponents; however, we can vary our bet sizes based on other factors – such as how strong we perceive our opponent's hand to be. If we believe our opponent's hand to be relatively weak, we can make our value bet on the river rather small, hoping to induce a call. If we believe (or hope) our opponents have a strong hand, we can make our river bet larger, and still hope to get a call.

Effectively, this means that our bets with stronger hands will, on average, be larger than other with weaker hands we're also value betting (since, if we suspect our opponent is strong enough to call a large bet, we wouldn't bet without a strong hand of our own). Against most opponents in $1/$2 games, there's no need to worry about this; our bets are still somewhat mixed, and they're unlikely to pick up on any batters (especially if you're not playing with the same players again and again).

However, if you're playing against some tougher opponents on occasion, there is a way to still utilize this mixed bet-sizing strategy without becoming predictable. Since you'll be bluffing more frequently against these tough, aggressive opponents, you can simply make your bluffs, on average, larger than normal bets as well. This will effectively mix your bets of all sizes: smaller bets could signify either a marginally strong hand or a monster, while larger bets represent a more polarized range: either you hold a monster (again) or a bluff.

An example from the WSOP

One great example of how large bets on the river can extract value came from a recent tournament hand. In the later stages of the 2011 World Series of Poker Main Event, two players who would ultimately make the final table – Ben Lamb and Matt Giannetti – played a very dramatic hand. With the blinds at 150,000/300,000 and a 40,000 ante, Lamb raised from the cutoff for 675,000. All other players folded to Giannetti, who called from the big blind. The flop came:

A♥ 9♥ 2♦

Giannetti checked the flop, and Lamb bet 700,000. Giannetti quickly called.

The turn card was the **7♦**. Giannetti checked, and Lamb checked behind.

Finally, the river card came as the **2♥**. Giannetti checked, and with the pot standing at slightly over 3 million chips, Lamb pushed out a bet of 4 million! This sent Giannetti into a long think – clearly signifying that Giannetti had a hand with showdown value, but not a monster.

Lamb's bet was clearly a bet that represented a polarized range; either Lamb had a strong hand (trips or better), or he was on a total bluff, as Lamb would certainly not bet a marginal hand like **AQ** rather than take the free showdown.

After a ten minute think, Giannetti finally made the call. Lamb revealed **3♣ 2♠** for trip deuces. Given how long Giannetti had spent thinking about the hand, it was no surprise to see him muck his hand (which turned out to be A9 for top two pair).

Of course, it's rare that you'll be playing in a $1/$2 game that requires the kind of deep analysis both Lamb and Giannetti employed in that hand, and you should probably never take ten minutes to make a decision in a low-stakes game. That said, understanding how varying your river bet sizes to fit the situation can earn you plenty of additional money in no-limit games of any level.

KEY POINTS

- Only bet the river if you can conceivably get a weaker hand to call, or a stronger hand to fold.

- With marginal hands, checking the river and attempting to get to a showdown for free is usually the best play.

- If your opponent may have a strong hand that you can still beat, making a larger river bet is a great way to extract additional value. If your opponent likely has a weak-to-marginal hand, a smaller bet may instead illicit a crying call.

PLAYING DRAWS

Draws are often misplayed by weak or new players, and interestingly, they can be misplayed in a variety of different ways. Some of the most common mistakes made when playing draws include:

- Playing draws too transparently
- Overestimating the strength of weak draws
- Underestimating the strength of strong draws
- Choosing to semi-bluff at the wrong times, or with the wrong draws

Playing draws well is an important skill in no-limit hold'em, since many of your biggest pots will come in situations where you make a straight or a flush – and in most of these cases, you'll likely flop a draw that you later make on the turn or river. Misplayed draws, then, can cost you money in two ways: you might cost yourself a large pot you should have won by folding (or putting yourself in a position where you have to fold), or you can put big bets into a pot when you shouldn't.

Luckily, there are some general rules that can be followed that will allow you to play draws without making the kinds of major errors that are so common in $1/$2 games. Keep these tips in mind, and you'll find that you'll get paid off more often when you hit your draws, and lose less of your stack when they don't.

The Power (and Danger) of Implied Odds

Clearly, implied odds are critical to the value of our drawing hands. While we'll sometimes be lucky enough to have the immediate odds necessary to make our draws profitable (or even get free cards from our passive opponents), there will be many times in which you are clearly being laid a price that isn't good enough to immediately justify a call. For instance, if an opponent bets $25 into a $50 pot on the flop, and you hold a flush draw, your immediate pot odds are 3-1 (the pot is now $75, and you must call $25). Since you're a little worse than 4-1 to make your flush on the next card, the pot odds would suggest that you can't call.

But, of course, we all know that's not true, thanks to the implied odds. In most cases, your implied odds will be strong enough to make up the difference and swing this situation from a fold to a call (or even a raise). Since our draws will usually collect some money after they hit, we can count on doing at least a little better than our pot odds would dictate. If the additional money we expect to win when we hit our draw is enough (combined with the money already in the pot) to make our draw profitable, then we won't want to fold.

Calculating implied odds is an inexact science at best. We also need to consider our reverse implied odds – the money we may pay off later in the hand if we don't win. These two concepts are closely related; in fact, you can think of them as two parts of the same equation, pulling you in opposite directions. While it's impossible to precisely calculate your implied or reverse-implied odds, you can make a quick checklist of factors that will help point you in the right direction:

- **Effective Stack Size:** Stack size is a limiting factor on the implied odds you might be receiving (or giving to an opponent). Obviously, the effective stack is the most you can win in any given hand; the deeper the stacks, the better your implied odds might be. At the other extreme, if the action will be moving all-in on the current round of betting, there are absolutely no implied odds to worry about; if another player moves all-in when you hold a draw, you must simply consider what kind of equity you likely have, and decide whether or not your pot odds are sufficient to make a call.
- **Draw Strength:** Draws to the nuts (or close to the nuts) tend to have better implied odds than draws that can potentially be beat. There's a simple reason for this: when you are drawing to a hand that isn't a guaranteed winner, you will occasionally make your draw only to lose to a better hand. In addition, a weak draw has fewer strong hands that it can beat, meaning fewer hands are out there that will be willing to pay off your draw. The weaker your draw is (in relation to the strongest possible hand), the more your implied odds are weakened.
- **Draw Obviousness:** If it's obvious that a likely draw just came in, even weak players are going to think twice before paying off a big bet later in the hand. On the other

hand, a draw that isn't likely to be noticed by your opponents has much more potential to be paid off. Most flush draws are rather transparent; however, some straight draws can easily be overlooked, especially if your opponents aren't likely to think you could hold those hands. For instance, if you held 85 in the big blind and the flop came A67, you're likely to be paid off should you make your draw – especially if the turn is a 4.

- **Board Texture:** Even if your particular draw isn't obvious, players are going to be less likely to pay you off if there's a wet board and many draws are possible. If you hold a relatively weak draw on a wet board, your reverse implied odds also go up, since you could easily draw to a second-best hand.

- **Our Opponents' Hands:** If our opponents are likely to be on strong hands, they'll be more apt to call our future bets than if they're weak, in which case they're likely to fold. The better you become as a hand reader, the better you'll be able to apply this factor in your decision making.

- **Player Strength:** Simply put, weaker players are more likely to pay off with the second best hand than stronger players are. If you're a better player than your opponent, you can figure to get a little more out of your implied odds; if you're up against tough opponents, don't count on them making big mistakes if you make your draw.

- **Number of Opponents:** This one is pretty obvious; your implied odds go up with more opponents in the hand, though this is also true for your reverse implied odds. If you're drawing to a weak hand, having many opponents could be a discouraging factor; however, for most draws, having multiple opponents will generally improve your odds of being paid off.

All of this might seem like a lot to consider, but you don't need to be precise in figuring out exactly what your implied odds are. The idea is simply to try to figure out whether or not conditions are favorable for you to attempt to continue drawing to a hand, or whether doing so might be a losing proposition in the long run. If the factors seem to point towards things being favorable for your draw, you might be able to call some fairly significant bets and still expect to make a profit on the play. On the other hand, if these factors are looking unfavorable for you, it may be best to throw away your hand unless you can proceed cheaply.

Semi-Bluffing with Draws

When we play draws, there are two main ways we can go about doing so. We can play passively, hoping to win a big pot if we happen to hit our draw, or we can aggressively semi-bluff, giving ourselves two ways to win the pot: we can take it down now if our opponents fold, or we could still win if we hit our draw.

While we spend most of this book extolling the virtues of playing aggressively, the semi-bluff with a draw is actually one place where it's easy to go overboard and use it too often. In fact, playing a draw passively is often correct, especially if you have a strong draw. Sure, you can make continuation bets with a lot of your draws if you were the preflop raiser, of course, and draws that are combined with a value hand (such as having top pair and a flush draw) can be played in much the same way you would any top pair hand, only with the added advantage that you have an unexpected way to improve.

But for most other draws, you'll want to think carefully before going for a semi-bluff. There are three major factors that should dissuade you from choosing to semi-bluff: having a draw that is likely to hit, having a draw to a strong hand (like the nuts), and having strong implied odds. Luckily, these factors tend to go hand-in-hand most of the time, so it's usually fairly obvious when you have a hand that's probably not worth turning into a semi-bluff.

The reasoning here is that these strong draws are the hands that benefit least from the fold equity you'll get by making a bluff. Making a stab at the pot early in the hand cuts into your implied odds (as your opponents might just fold immediately), and since you're often going to make your hand, that could cost you a good deal of money in the long run. In addition, should your opponent surprise you by making a big raise over your semi-bluff, you might be put into a position where you may have to fold a hand that had significant equity in the pot – which is never a fun position to find yourself in.

On the other hand, weak draws make for excellent semi-bluffs. Now, the fold equity greatly improves your chances of winning in the hand, since hitting your draw is relatively unlikely. If your opponents do call, you still have at least a few outs to the best hand – and your bet means your opponents are far less likely to think you have a draw when you do hit.

Monster Draws

Some draws are so strong that they can be considered favorites even against rather strong made hands. For instance, consider holding **K♣ Q♣** on a board of **4♠ T♣ J♣**. You probably realize you have a big draw, but the combination of flush and straight draws with two overcards actually means you have a monster. Just look at your hand's chances of being best at showdown against some possible hands you might be up against:

A♦ J♦ : 67%
J♥ T♥ : 53%
A♥ A♠ : 49%
4♦ 4♣ : 42%

That's right: even against a made set, you're barely worse than a coin flip! Granted, your draw isn't exactly hidden, so your implied odds may suffer somewhat here. But your hand is strong enough to bet simply for value, let alone any future bets you may win.

For the most part, monster draws can be played aggressively, since unlike some other draws, you won't be afraid of getting a lot of money into the pot with them now. In fact, it may be advantageous in many cases to get the money in on the flop with a monster draw, since this will guarantee you will get to see both remaining cards and get to a showdown. On the other hand, there is something to be said for seeing the next card; if you hit your draw, your equity obviously goes way up, while if you're still on a draw, the value of your hand is somewhat diminished.

This is a good spot for mixing up your play when your opponent bets into you: sometimes raising for value, and other times, calling to see what the turn will bring. Of course, you don't have to do this randomly, especially against weak opponents! If you think you're up against a player who is very likely to pay you off if you hit your draw – and these players are hardly rare in low-stakes games – then playing a monster draw more passively can make some sense. If, on the other hand, you think your implied odds aren't that great (either because of the way your opponents play, the board texture, or the fact that the effective stacks are short), it's likely better to get your money in now, and hopefully ride your draw's monster potential to a win (or take down a smaller pot now). As always in no-limit hold'em, your perception of your implied odds will often dictate your play in these situations.

KEY POINTS

- Draws can be played passively, in the hopes of hitting your hand, or aggressively, as a semi-bluff.
- Generally, the better your implied odds, the more likely it will be right to play the hand passively.
- Monster draws are big hands that are often favorites at showdown against even strong "made" hands like top pair or two pair.

HAND READING AND OUT THINKING YOUR OPPONENTS

In general, weak players are very poor at reading hands – if they even attempt to do so at all. Many players barely give a second thought to their opponents' hands; one common approach among many poor players (and even some average ones) is to only start to consider what their opponents might hold when they're faced with a big decision. Another popular way of "hand reading" is to just put every single opponent on ace-king. If you don't believe this is actually a real phenomenon, just try to Google "I put him on AK" and be astonished at the number of results you get!

To be honest, you don't have to do a lot of complex hand reading doing low-stakes no-limit. In fact, trying too hard to outthink your opponents can actually get you in trouble, as it could lead you to some faulty conclusions. That said, it's always a good idea to try to figure out the range of hands your opponents could be on, since it'll help your decision-making process immensely. Even against weak opponents, there are plenty of situations where have an idea of what your opponents might be holding can affect your play – particularly when you're faced with an all-in situation, and on the river when you're trying to figure out whether or not a value bet (or a call) would be profitable.

Given that hand reading is a pretty advanced topic, we're not going to go into anything overly complex here. With a general understanding of the different levels of thinking in poker, along with a few basic hand reading techniques, you should be able to learn enough about your opponents' holdings to help your decision making process.

Levels of Thinking

Before we get down to hand reading, it's important to first talk about the thought process you'll want to be using at the table. Obviously, we want to outthink our opponents at the poker table; however, it's important only to do this to the proper extent. If you attempt to think incredibly deep about a hand in which your opponents aren't thinking beyond their own hand, you're likely to come to some faulty conclusions.

The depth of our thinking can generally be classified into different levels. Of course, it's quite possibly to think somewhere in between these levels; however, most players will tend towards thinking on a particular level on the majority of hands.

Level 1: On this level, a player is simply thinking about their own hand. They will consider how strong their hand is, and may even consider whether there are a number of possible stronger hands given the board. Many of your weak opponents will spend a lot of time on this level, occasionally jumping up to Level 2 (but not necessarily doing a good job of it).

Level 2: A level two thinker will think both about their own hand, as well as the possible hands of their opponents. This doesn't mean that their hand reading skills are good; however, it does mean that they will at least try to consider their opponents' holdings when making decisions. A fair number of $1/$2 players are on this level, at least some of the time.

Level 3: A level three thinker will consider their own hand, of course, as well as their opponents' hands. However, they will also consider what their opponents might be putting them on, as well, and attempt to use those perceptions against their opponents. This is often the default starting level for tough players, especially if they believe they'll be playing against generally weaker (but not unthinking) opponents.

Beyond level three, there are (in a theoretical sense) an unlimited number of higher levels in which you might try to outthink your opponents. For instance, **Level 4 thinking** would require you to consider what your opponents might think you're putting them on; on **Level 5**, you'd be thinking about what your opponents think that you think they're putting you on.

Obviously, thinking on the higher levels can quickly give you a headache. What many players fail to realize is that it's also completely unnecessary, and can lead you to the wrong conclusions. In order for your thinking to be effective against a given opponent, you'll ideally be thinking exactly one level above them. If you do that, you'll be correctly reacting to their thought process – as every level of thinking essentially says "my opponent on the previous level of thought is considering all of these things: what is my best response?"

Thus, the higher levels of thinking usually only come into play when very tough players play against each other, and explain what otherwise might seem like outlandish bluffs or incredibly silly calls to an outside observer. In a $1/$2 game, you'll likely spend most of your time defaulting to Level 2 or Level 3 thinking, adjusting based on whether or not your opponents appear to actually be thinking about what you hold (and actually using that information – curiously, you'll run into some players who think about what you have, but rarely use that information in their decision making).

In case the levels of thinking still sound like complete gibberish, here's a quick look at how one preflop situation might vary depending on what level you think on, and what level you think your opponents are on.

*You raise from middle position to **$10** with **A♥Q♥**. A late position player reraises to **$30**. All other players fold to you. You have **$90** behind, and have decided you will either fold or move all-in.*

Level 1 Thinking: *I have a strong hand that plays well all-in. I'm all-in!*

Level 2 Thinking: *My hand is strong, but my opponent is a tight-passive player. He would only three-bet here with **AK** or **99+**. I am way behind that range; I'll fold.*

Level 3 Thinking: *My hand is strong, but my opponent is a tight-passive player. He would only three-bet here with **AK** or **99+**. However, I know that he'll put me on **AA** or **KK** if I make a four-bet all-in; in fact, I'm sure he'd only call the bet with **AA** or **KK**. I'll make enough money*

on the times he folds to show a profit, even though I'm only **25%** *to win if he calls. I'm all-in.*

As you can see, your thinking quickly grows in complexity as you reach the higher levels. In addition, that example shows why thinking on too high of a level is dangerous; were you thinking on Level 3 when your opponent was only on Level 1, you would come to the wrong conclusion, as your opponent would likely snap call with most of the hands in his range. The key is to think more than your opponents too – but only by a little.

Tips for Hand Reading

Again, we're not going to delve too deeply into the more complex aspects of hand reading, as these will rarely be important at the $1/$2 level. However, basic hand reading is important; we want to be able to have some idea of what our opponents are holding. Since our opponents will often basically be playing their hands face up, this doesn't take too much effort – once we know what to look for. Here are a few of the most critical things to watch for:

- **Opponent Tendencies:** The type of player you're up against is the first general way to narrow down an opponent's holdings. A tight-passive player's range begins extremely tightly, while a loose-passive player could have just about any combination of hands. Tough players might have wide ranges, but will generally have at least reasonable speculative hands (in other words, 6♣4♣ is a more likely holding for a tough player than T♣3♥ in most situations). As you play with your opponents more, you'll develop more specific guidelines on an individual basis; you may find certain players who will play any ace, any two face cards, or particular favorite hands, for instance. Most importantly, know if your opponent is a straightforward player (common in low-stakes games) that you can easily put on a range, or a tricky or tough player who will be more difficult to read.
- **Preflop Action:** Even later in a hand, it's always wise to go back to the preflop action and see what that might tell you about what your opponent could be holding. Most of your opponents in $1/$2 games will play relatively straightforward poker; they'll raise with their top hands, and limp with others. They'll also likely need to have at least a reasonable hand to call a raise. Most players are unlikely to hold **AA** if they limped into a pot after several other limpers; conversely, they're not likely to have made a raise or a three-bet with 5♥4♥. On the other hand, a player in the blinds in a limped pot might literally have any two cards.
- **Postflop Aggression:** In general, when a player in a $1/$2 game shows you aggression after the flop, you can be sure that they have a hand. Sure, you'll have some opponents who just love to bluff; but if you don't have any information on an opponent, or you think that they fit our mold of the typical loose-passive player, then a raise or a bet is a sure sign of strength. Check-raises are even more obvious indicators, and typically signify a set or better from most weak players (though it's not impossible for even weak players to occasionally make this play with a strong drawing hand). If a player makes a big bet, that's almost always a sign that they're holding a strong hand, even if that means they must have a hand you previously thought impossible; don't outthink yourself and try to justify a loose call when it will cost you a lot of money (in relation to the size of the pot).
- **Transparent Draws:** If a loose-passive player checks and calls on a flop that contains a draw, that draw hits on the next card (or on the river), and they then switch to betting or check-raising, it's a pretty safe bet that they've made that

draw. The though process from a weak player here is obvious; they're going to stay in the hand as cheaply as possible, and then make their move once they're sure they have the best hand. Again, against stronger players, this read won't be as reliable; a good, aggressive player is capable of making a bluff in this spot, knowing that the possible straight or flush may scare you away.

- **Physical Tells:** Physical tells aren't going to be a big topic of discussion in this book, but they do play a role in hand reading. Basically, if you're up against a weak player who doesn't even notice you're paying attention to them, take the demeanor of your opponent at face value; if they seem like an actor instead, go by the mantra that "strong means weak, weak means strong." If you can get a reliable read on your opponent based on some physical sign, that can go a long way towards putting your opponent on a hand – but you should use these tells **only in conjunction with the action in a hand**. In other words, if everything that happened in a hand and everything you know about a player tells you that they have to be strong, don't assume they're bluffing just because they've done something that you think signifies weakness. For more information on physical tells, there are a number of great book recommendations in the appendix!

Essentially, hand reading is the process of figuring out what hand makes sense based on everything you've seen in the hand. The goal is to take all of that information and use it to come up with a range of hands our opponent might be on. An important note here: **We do not have to put our opponents on exact hands!** As long as we can narrow our opponents' holdings, we're reducing our uncertainty and will correspondingly improve our results in the long run. As you improve, you'll find your ability to read hands allows you to occasionally call out a hand with extreme accuracy, and that you can more reliably narrow your opponents' ranges to a few hands. But to start out, it's more important to be accurate in our hand reading than extremely precise; it's better to give your opponent a wide range that actually includes his hand than a narrow range that doesn't.

One last tip: if you're facing a bet and your opponent's line simply doesn't make sense no matter what hand they might have, and they've shown themselves to be capable of bluffing in the past, you should seriously consider the idea that they might be bluffing here. Bad players often bluff in spots where it doesn't make sense; however, their value bets tend to be relatively straightforward. This doesn't mean you should assume they're bluffing every time you don't understand their play, but it's at least worth some consideration.

A Basic Hand Reading Example

A tight-passive player limps in early position. You're up next, and raise to $10 with A♣K♣. The table folds around to the early position limper, who calls. You both have around $300 behind. The pot is $23, and the flop comes:

7♣ 3♠ 5♥

The player checks to you, and you make a continuation bet of $15. Your opponent instantly calls. The pot is up to $53, and the turn is:

J♣

Your opponent checks. With two overcards and a flush draw, you decide to semi-bluff, and

bet *$30. Once again, your opponent calls nearly instantly. The pot is now $113. The river is an A♠, making the final board:*

7♣ 3♠ 5♥ J♣ A♠

Your opponent throws out a bet of $80 on the river. What do you do?

Before we decide on our action, we have to put our opponent on a hand. We know our opponent is tight-passive, which likely tells us three things about their hand right off the top:

- Our opponent is probably not bluffing on the river.
- Our opponent had to have a reasonable hand preflop.
- Our opponent had to have hit the flop somehow to call our flop and turn bets.

Factor one should tell us that our opponent has at least a pair, thus eliminating all busted draws like **8♣6♣**, which would have been an unlikely hand for a tight-passive player to play preflop anyway. A tight-passive player might choose to play big suited cards, big unsuited cards, and pocket pairs. They may go a little deeper with suited hands, but probably not down to the small one-gappers that would make a straight draw possible – or for that matter, a straight itself. Maybe a hand like **A♦4♦** would be possible, since it would at least give our opponent a draw on the flop, and a made hand on the river; however, it's not a hand all tight-passive players would even consider playing against a raise. Still, we can't eliminate it entirely.

Pocket pairs are also possible. Our opponent might have limped and called with a hand like **88, 99,** or **TT**. However, that wouldn't explain their river play; in those cases, our opponent would be expected to check/call or perhaps even check/fold against a scary ace, and they might even think we have a jack. On the other hand, a pair like **JJ** or higher seems unlikely as well; even tight players will usually raise with those hands.

So, what does that leave us with? How about a set? Our opponent could easily have limped and called a raise with any of **77, 55,** or **33**. With such a strong hand, they might have checked the flop to the preflop raiser, then given us another chance to take the lead when the jack hit the board. On the river, the ace will improve our hand a good percentage of the time; our opponent might think that could lead us to call a bet should we improve.

In fact, a set is by far the most likely hand here, given our opponent and the action (even our opponents' quick calls might be a sign that he was strong). Against a truly tight-passive opponent, we can probably safely fold here; even though we can't put them on an exact hand, we can combine all the factors in our analysis to say they likely made a set on the flop. Against more aggressive opponents, we'd likely have to call, as bluffing at the river ace would make sense for them (though they'll often have us beat, too).

KEY POINTS

- If possible, we'd like to always think one level above our opponents.

- Outthinking ourselves against unthinking opponents can cause us to make mistakes.

- Reading hands is an important skill. However, we don't need to put our opponents on an exact hand; instead, we should use everything we know about the action and our opponents to narrow their holdings down to a likely range.

BLUFFS

There's an old joke about a player who shows up to a poker table with a book titled *How to Win at Poker by Bluffing*. They sit down, clean out the table, and then leave with their winnings – but apparently forget their book, leaving it behind. One of their bewildered opponents grabs the book and opens it up, finding just a single word printed inside:

"DON'T!"

It's a cute joke, but horrible advice for most no-limit hold'em games. Without bluffing at all, opponents will quickly pick up on your tendencies, and be able to narrow your holdings very easily. Essentially, you'll be playing with your cards face up against good opponents, since you're not even attempting to use any deception in your game.

On the other hand, the $1/$2 games we're playing in are filled with players who, by and large, do not fold nearly often enough with poor hands. That's a bad environment for bluffing; if your bluffs are being called too often, they quickly become unprofitable. On the other hand, players who don't fold are easy to exploit; that's why most of this book has been primarily about how to extract the most value from your good hands.

That said, there are quite a few spots where you'll want to run bluffs even in low-limit games. We've already talked about continuation bets, which are often bluffs (or semi-bluffs) designed to win a hand not based on the strength of what you hold, but by getting your opponents to fold.

Against passive opponents – especially tight-passive opponents – there will be plenty of "dead money" pots postflop where it becomes clear that your opponents have no interest in winning the hand. This will allow you to pick up plenty of hands in which you don't have a hand – but it's likely that your opponents don't either. Here's an example:

A player in early position limps. A middle position, you call with 9♥7♥. A tight-passive player in late position raises to $8. Everyone folds to the limper, who calls; you also call, making the pot $27 heading to the flop. The flop comes:

T♣ 8♦ 3♥

After the early position player and you both check, the preflop raiser makes a continuation bet of $15. The player in early position folds, but you call, hoping to hit your straight draw. The pot is now $57. The turn comes:

3♦

You check again. This time, the preflop raiser checks back. The river is the 4♣, making the final board:

T♣ 8♦ 3♥ 3♦ 4♣

This is an excellent place to fire out a reasonably sized bluff – say, a bet of $40. It is unlikely that your opponent improved on the river, and it seems that your flop call was enough to make them slow down. Your opponent is a tight-passive player; that limits their potential holdings somewhat. They might have an overpair, but it's very unlikely that most weak players would slow down in this situation with **JJ** or better. Similarly, it's unlikely that such a tight-passive player would raise with a medium or small pocket pair; they're much more likely to have limped behind with a hand like **77**.

Instead, a much more likely holding is **AK** or **AQ** (or two other big cards), which is the kind of hand a tight player might raise with preflop, throw out a continuation bet with, but then give up on against any resistance. You can't beat this hand at showdown, of course – but your opponent is also very unlikely to call here with just ace-high. While they'll occasionally come up with a hand that can call you, your bluff is likely to work more than half the time; since a two-thirds pot size bet will only have to work about 40% of the time to break even, this play is almost certainly profitable in this spot.

This should help you realize the kind of spot where a bluff is obviously the correct play. In $1/$2 games, that's really the only spot in which you need to bluff regularly; while there are plenty of other times in which bluffs might be profitable, it's not necessary to constantly run big bluffs to win in these games.

With that in mind, we're going to stop talking about bluffing now. Bluffing too often in a $1/$2 game is a much bigger leak than bluffing too little, so it's much better if you err towards failing to find spots to bluff rather than finding excuses to bluff in situations where it is entirely unwarranted. In tougher games, bluffing in the proper spots is a critical skill that's necessary to keep your play unpredictable and balance your ranges; in a $1/$2 game, you can reliably win simply by value betting your opponents to death. If you're following the advice provided throughout this book, your game will feature enough deception for a small stakes game without requiring any audacious moves on your part.

KEY POINTS

- The environment in most $1/$2 games is not ideal for frequent bluffing.

- There are spots in which it is right to bluff, particularly when opponents have clearly given up on pots.

- When playing in small stakes games, it's far better to bluff too little than to bluff too often.

CHECK-RAISES

Check-raises have a certain mystique to them in poker. Once upon a time, they were seen as unsportsmanlike by many players, to the point where the check-raise was outlawed in most home games. These days, where trickiness has become commonplace in poker, many players have moved in the opposite direction, looking to check-raise every time they make a good hand out of position.

The truth is that the check-raise should just be another tool you can use when it is appropriate to do so. For the most part, the check-raise is a move that's far trickier than necessary when playing in a typical $1/$2 game. In most cases, you'll be better served by making a bet than attempting a check-raise, for two key reasons:

- Passive players are likely to check behind you, thus avoiding your trap (and often giving the opponent a free card if they're on a draw that can beat you).
- Likewise, passive players will call you down often enough that you'll get plenty of value from your big hands simply by betting them.

These two reasons combine to make betting a much more lucrative play than check-raising in most situations. However, there are a few specific spots where you'll definitely want to incorporate the check-raise into your game.

When to Check-Raise

There are at least two situations in which check-raising in a $1/$2 game makes sense. The first comes when you hit a flop well out-of-position against a preflop raiser. For instance, imagine the following hand:

One player limps in early position. A player in late position raises to **$10**. *All fold to you in the big blind, where you hold* **A♥Q♥**. *You decide to call, and the limper folds. The pot is now* **$23**, *and the flop comes:*

7♠ 4♣ Q♦

In this situation, you will likely have the best hand, but one that isn't strong enough to slow play. You could lead out with a bet, and this wouldn't be a major mistake. However, even weak opponents understand the normal flow of a hand, and that it's typical for players to check to the preflop raiser. If you bet, you might get a call, but a fair percentage of the time, your opponent will fold if they didn't hit the flop (or have an overpair).

Instead, it might be a better idea to check to your opponent here, especially if you know they have a tendency to make continuation bets a fair percentage of the time. Your opponent is likely to bet to try to win the pot right there. Now you can go for a check-raise. Most of the time, you'll win the pot right there; if your opponent calls, you can go into a defensive shell (and if they reraise, you can feel confident that you're up against a monster). Here's how it might play out in the above hand:

You check the flop. Your opponent makes a continuation bet of **$15**. *With a pot of* **$38**, *you make a check-raise to* **$45**. *Your opponent folds, and you rake in the pot.*

These sorts of check-raises can be made any time you expect an opponent to make a routine and predictable bet. While the continuation bet is the most common of these types of bets, they can occur on later streets as well. For instance, if you check-call an opponent on the flop and hit a non-obvious draw, you may be able to check-raise on the turn – and often even get called, since your opponent may not believe that you have the oddball straight draw or suddenly improved to trips.

In addition, you may sometimes wish to check-raise the flop in an unraised multiway plot. If you flop a hand that is vulnerable but strong (such as top pair, good kicker), and you are one of the first players to act with at least a couple more players behind you, you may wish to check, hoping for a bet behind you. Since a single bet in a pot like this is unlikely to win the pot outright (weak and passive players are likely to call a small flop bet if they hit any part of the board), and your hand is vulnerable when facing several opponents who could all be looking to improve, a check-raise may be a more effective way of taking down the pot. For example:

An early position player limps, and you limp behind with **A♦9♦**. *Two more players limp behind you, and both blinds stay in the pot as well, sending six players to the flop with a* **$12** *pot. The flop comes:*

3♠ 9♥ 7♦

If the action is checked to you, it's probably best to check through. While you probably have the best hand, it's very vulnerable, and an $8-$10 bet is unlikely to knock out a loose-passive player with anything resembling a draw; a fair number of players will call with two overcards. Instead, if you can get one of the players behind you to bet that $8 or so, you can then make a sizable reraise (perhaps to the range of $25), likely taking the pot down right there. Even if you get a single caller, you now have a much more manageable situation on the turn.

One final place to go for these check-raises is against habitual bluffers, especially on the river. While they do not fit the mold of the "common" opponent at the $1/$2 tables, there will be some opponents who just love making tricky plays (including plenty of check-raises of their own). If you're out-of-position with a very strong hand on the river against one of these players, it may be best to check to them in the hopes of inducing a bluff, and then punish them with a check-raise. However, this is only worthwhile against a particular type of opponent – the tricky opponent who is more likely to bet the river after you check rather than call a bet you make yourself. Most of your opponents will not fit this mold, so be sure about who you're up against before trying this.

KEY POINTS

- The dynamics of most $1/$2 games make the check-raise less effective than in tougher games.

- Check-raises can be used in certain circumstances, such as when you are out-of-position and flop a good hand against a player who reliably makes continuation bets.

- Check-raises can also be strong against habitual bluffers, though these players are uncommon in small-stakes games.

PART IV: ADDITIONAL ADVICE

MISCELLANEOUS TIPS

There are a number of ideas that didn't fit neatly into one of the previous chapters, but which are still valuable to know when playing small-stakes no-limit poker. These tips are very important to keep in mind while playing, and will go a long way towards helping you maintain an edge over your opponents at most soft no-limit tables.

• **Believe big bets.** There are lots of tough no-limit opponents out there who are willing and able to make large bluffs, even to the point of over-betting the pot with nothing if they think they'll get you to fold. However, these opponents are rarely (if ever) playing in $1/$2 games. If your opponents make a big bet on one of the later streets – especially if they are the common, weak loose-passive opponents we've described to you throughout this book – then it's time to give them credit for a hand. Will they occasionally bluff you like this? Yes, on rare occasions, even the most solid player will be running a bluff. But most of the time, it's correct to give them credit for a real hand, and react accordingly. What yoou do in reaction, of course, will depend on the strength of your own hand.

• **Don't raise if you don't know what to do if your opponent will reraise.** If you make a raise knowing that you'll fold to a reraise, that's fine; that's often the case with bluffs, for instance. If you raise with a very strong hand and plan to get all the money in (or at least call) if your opponent reraises, that's great too. The situation you don't want to find yourself in is raising with a modest hand that has showdown value, but doesn't necessarily want to call a reraise. If you have a hand like top pair, top kicker, and are facing aggression from an opponent who acts before you, it's okay to simply make a call on the flop. Depending on the situation and the opponent, you might even be willing to call bets on the turn and river, too. While playing aggressively is correct more often than not, no-limit hold'em does have situations in which playing passively is correct; don't be aggressive for the sake of aggression in situations where it's clearly not warranted.

• **It's okay to call a bet, planning to fold to another bet.** This is related to the last point. While in some cases you may be willing to call down all the way against aggression, there will be other times where a call is clearly correct – and yet your hand isn't nearly strong enough to stay in against bets on every street. That's okay! The fact that your opponent bets once doesn't necessarily mean they will continue betting; if they do, that's additional information that you've learned about their hand. There are many players out there who will occasionally show aggression, but get scared the minute someone calls a bet; these players may well check the turn after betting the flop, making your vulnerable or marginal hand much easier to play, since you can more easily reach a cheap showdown. If they bet again, on the other hand, that usually signals real strength, and you may have to fold many modest hands.

• **Unless you have a huge hand, don't play a big pot against a very tight or very good player.** Against very tight players, you can feel certain that they'll never put all of their money in the pot without an extremely strong hand. Thus, you'd better have a big hand to play against them in these situations – preferably the nuts, or something close to it. Similarly, if you're up against a player who is much better than you, it's probably best to avoid playing large pots with them unless you're holding a hand you feel confident will win at showdown; with more marginal hands, you can minimize your risk of being outplayed by trying to keep the pot small and refusing to stack off with a second-best hand.

- **If you're not sure what to bet, err high, not low.** Earlier in the book, we talked about preflop bet sizing, and said to start on the lower-end of what is commonly bet at most $1/$2 tables. However, that's only because $1/$2 preflop raises tend to be too large (in a theoretical sense) in general; therefore bets towards the bottom of this range are less likely to be exploited by your opponents. When it comes to postflop betting, however, it's better to bet a little too much than slightly too little. If you're making a value bet, your loose-passive opponents aren't likely to base their decision to call or not based on the exact amount you bet, so getting a few extra dollars of value is a no-brainer. Similarly, if you're running a bluff against a player who does consider bet sizing, betting a little bit too much might get a fold you wouldn't otherwise get. This doesn't mean you should be making big bets all the time; what it means is that, if you've decided that a bet of between $40-$50 is proper in a given situation but aren't sure where in that range is absolutely collect, it's usually best to make that bet closer to $50.

- **It's okay to just flat call a raise with a strong hand preflop.** For instance, imagine you have AA in late position. If someone opens with a raise to $10, and there are no callers, just calling behind is sometimes fine – especially if you think your opponents are perceptive about your normal three-betting habits, or the raiser is very unlikely to call a three-bet. This play can be done with any big hand, but if you're uncomfortable with it, it's easiest to do with aces; there's no flop that can immediately make aces feel uncomfortable (whereas a hand like KK or QQ is a little harder to play if an overcard comes).

- **Don't overcall with marginal hands that aren't likely to improve.** If you have top pair with a modest kicker on the flop, you'd normally like to continue on here – either by betting out, or calling/raising a bettor who gets into the pot before you. However, the situation changes if you're dealing with multiple opponents who have already chosen to continue on in the pot. For instance, if you hold a fair top-pair hand, but see a raise and a call in front of you, you'll often have to let this hand go (or if you're feeling cheeky and your opponents tend to fold a lot, try to take it down right there with a raise). While your hand is good, it's unlikely to beat both a bettor and a caller – and it's even less likely that you'll have any confidence in your hand if betting continues on later streets. Remember, the first player bet into multiple players, knowing a call was possible, which shows strength; another player then made a call, which also shows at least some strength. Unless you have the combination of an aggressive bettor and an extremely loose-passive caller (or callers), you probably don't want to get involved with a hand that's extremely unlikely to improve. However, a strong draw is a fine hand to continue with here; having multiple opponents improves both your pot odds and your implied odds. Conversely, you should be wary of players who overcall your bets; while it's not as much of an indicator as in tougher games, even most $1/$2 players won't overcall without some kind of a hand.

- **Don't tap the glass or berate players.** This one is about table demeanor. When you're playing against weak opponents, you want to keep things as friendly as possible. Most of your opponents aren't professionals; they're there to have a good time, gamble it up, and socialize with their fellow players. Anything that makes the atmosphere more serious will tend to tighten the table up, and make players focus more on playing well – which is exactly what you don't want. With that in mind, don't get mad at a player who gets lucky and beats you by hitting their miracle card on the river – and whatever you do, don't tell them how they should have played. If they believe you, you've just made one of your opponents better, and made them aware that you're a smart player that they need to pay more attention to. If they take offense at your comment, the mood of the whole table will come down, and that's likely to have an unpleasant effect on the game. On a similar note, there's no need to wear sunglasses at a $1/$2 table; none of your opponents are trying to read your soul, but you might scare some of your casual opponents who otherwise would have had a few drinks and built you big pots.

• **As the hand goes on, your bets should get smaller in relation to the pot.** This isn't always true, especially in the weak games we talk about; you may easily get away with making pot size bets on every street against a weak opponent who hates to fold any made hand. But even against most mediocre opponents, you'll want to tone down the size of your bets as the hand goes on. Note that the absolute size of your bets will be going up; it's just the percentage of the pot you're betting that will diminish. You don't have to bet as much on later streets to get the same job done; your opponents get weaker implied odds from you on the turn than they did on the flop, and on the river, there are no implied odds to worry about at all. On the river, in fact, it may sometimes be correct to make a very small bet, if you think that's all your opponent could possibly call in your situation. However, remember that this is only a general guideline, and not an ironclad rule; there are certainly times when a big bet is correct on the turn and/or river.

• **Always pay attention to your opponents' bet sizing, even if it tells you nothing about the strength of their hand.** Some opponents will transparently size their bets, making pot-sized bets with strong hands and betting far less with weak hands. Still others will vary their bet sizes for what appears to be no discernable reason (and sometimes, there really isn't any). In either case, you should pay attention to how much is bet, and be more willing to call small bets than large ones. It's an obvious point, but one that can get overlooked with all the other things we've talked about; you get better odds when your opponent bets less, which means you can call profitably with more hands. If that bet size clues you in to the strength of their hand, this effect is all the stronger.

• **Learn how to handle preflop all-in situations.** We didn't spend much time on these here, because they aren't extremely common in small-stakes no-limit; you'll see them more often in tournament play, where players are forced to make moves due to the increasing blinds and antes. However, knowledge of these situations can improve your edge against your opponents. Most books on poker theory will have charts that outline proper push/call strategy in these situations; as you improve your play, it's a great idea to use these charts to understand the math behind preflop all-ins. For now, remember that pairs and big cards play much better in all-in situations, while the speculative hands we love so much in deep-stack situations don't fare nearly as well. Calling a $20 all-in when you are the last to act with A♠7♥ is likely absolutely correct, though you'd probably never play this hand against a raise; meanwhile, a hand like 6♣5♣ is certainly not worth playing in this situation, as that hand would normally rely on implied odds to become profitable. For more information on this topic, check out some of the additional reading we recommend in the appendix to this book.

• **If you're playing online poker, remember that a $1/$2 game at an online site is not the same as a $1/$2 live game.** In reality, a $1/$2 online no-limit table is likely tougher than a typical live $2/$5 table, let alone a $1/$2 game. The difference is that a $1/$2 game is the "introductory" game in a live casino, while that role in an online poker room might be at stakes as low as $0.02/0.04. The advice in this book is most apt for microstakes online games, and even there, you should make a few adjustments. You're likely to see many, many more tight players at these tables than in live games; this doesn't mean that they're good, by and large, but you'll have to adjust your play accordingly.

APPENDIX: FURTHER READING

If you're interested in continuing to improve your poker game, you're in luck: there are plenty of excellent poker books out there that delve into advanced poker theory, or which talk about how to win in tough, high-stakes games. Here's a quick rundown of a few of the best:

The Theory of Poker (David Sklansky) – This book is a must read for any serious poker player; in fact, even if you never plan on playing a game other than $1/$2 no limit, it is well worth your time and money. This book doesn't focus on any particular poker game, instead talking about the underlying concepts that are important to all forms of poker. If you've ever wanted to truly understand the why behind poker theory, this book is the place to start.

No Limit Hold'em: Theory and Practice (David Sklansky, Ed Miller) – An excellent work that I referred to on many occasions when writing this book. As the title would suggest, there's a mix of theoretical background (including some heavy math) along with plenty of practical advice as well. While the book mostly talks about what you need to do to play against decent, thinking opponents, there is also information on how to beat loose games, as well as the weak/tight "nitty" games that you'll sometimes run into.

Small Stakes No-Limit Hold'em (Ed Miller, Sunny Mehta, Matt Flynn) – If you want to learn some deeper theoretical concepts for beating small stakes no-limit games, this is the book to jump into. It's especially useful if you want to take on online six-max games, which are a different beast entirely from $1/$2 live games.

ABOUT POKERSITES.COM

PokerSites.com was founded in 2001 as an online poker portal to provide visitors with a way to access information about regional poker play, popular deposit methods used and poker software. Today, PokerSites.com is the leading online portal for all things relating to Internet poker. Our site includes poker currency information, comparisons of some of the most popular online poker sites and information about the major poker games available at online poker rooms. Our poker room reviews and ratings help players to find the best poker sites online.

We have rated hundreds of online poker rooms across a huge variety of criteria. Whether you are looking for the sites with the most fish, or the fastest withdrawals, we have tested and listed our recommendations. That allows players to spend less time downloading and experimenting with sites, and more time playing at the tables.

At PokerSites.com we are all about you having a great experience when playing Internet poker. Our industry contacts and long experience allow us to help our readers resolve their problems as well. Although we know that, with the rooms we list, there should be almost none.

COME ON OVER TO POKERSITES.COM TODAY AND PUT YOUR SKILLS TO THE TEST!